The Essential
Ninja Foodi
Cookbook

1600 Days of Classic Recipes to Unlock a World of Healthy Cuisine | Full Color Edition

Cassandra A. Hoffman

Editor: LYN   **Interior Design:** FAIZAN
Cover Art: ABR   **Food stylist:** JO

Table Of Contents

Introduction

In today's fast-paced world, convenience and efficiency have become paramount in every aspect of our lives, including our approach to cooking. Enter the Ninja Foodi, a kitchen appliance that has taken the culinary world by storm with its innovative design and multifunctionality. Combining the power of a pressure cooker, air fryer, and more, the Ninja Foodi has become a game-changer for home cooks seeking to simplify their cooking routines and elevate their dishes to new heights.

At its core, the Ninja Foodi is a pressure cooker, offering the ability to cook meals in a fraction of the time compared to traditional methods. The Foodi's advanced pressure cooking technology allows for faster cooking while retaining the flavors and nutrients of your ingredients. Whether you're whipping up a tender roast, preparing a hearty soup, or experimenting with new recipes, the Ninja Foodi ensures consistently delicious results with minimal effort.

But the Ninja Foodi doesn't stop there. It also features the functionality of an air fryer, providing a healthier alternative to deep-frying your favorite foods. With its powerful crisping abilities, the Foodi can achieve that coveted golden-brown, crispy texture on everything from french fries and chicken wings to vegetables and even desserts. Say goodbye to excess oil and hello to guilt-free indulgence.

What sets the Ninja Foodi apart from other kitchen appliances is its versatility. It seamlessly transitions between cooking modes, allowing you to pressure cook, air fry, bake, roast, grill, and even dehydrate—all in one compact device. This versatility not only saves precious counter space but also opens up a world of culinary possibilities. Imagine being able to whip up a succulent steak, crispy potato wedges, and a delectable dessert all in one go.

The Ninja Foodi also features intuitive controls and a user-friendly interface, making it accessible to both experienced chefs and beginners alike. With its preset cooking functions and customizable settings, you have the flexibility to experiment with different flavors and cooking techniques without the fear of overcooking or undercooking.

The Ninja Foodi is a groundbreaking kitchen appliance that has transformed the way we cook. Its combination of a pressure cooker, air fryer, and numerous other cooking functions ensures convenience, efficiency, and exceptional results. Whether you're a busy professional, a health-conscious individual, or an aspiring chef, the Ninja Foodi is the ultimate tool to elevate your culinary creations to new heights. Get ready to revolutionize your cooking experience with the Ninja Foodi!

Chapter 1

Get Started with the Ninja Foodi

Navigating the Ninja Foodi

- A Step-by-Step Guide to Mastering Its Controls

The Ninja Foodi is a versatile and innovative kitchen appliance that can transform your cooking experience. To fully utilize its potential, it is essential to understand and master its controls. In this step-by-step guide, we will walk you through each aspect of the Ninja Foodi's controls, enabling you to harness its power and cook with confidence.

FAMILIARIZING YOURSELF WITH THE CONTROL PANEL

The control panel is the command center of your Ninja Foodi. Take a moment to acquaint yourself with its layout and buttons. Most models feature a digital display, power button, mode selection buttons, time and temperature adjustment buttons, start/stop button, and a keep warm function. Understanding these components will lay the foundation for navigating the controls effectively.

POWERING ON THE NINJA FOODI

Locate the power button on the control panel and press it to turn on the appliance. The digital display should light up, indicating that the Ninja Foodi is ready for use. If your model has a preheat function, allow it to preheat before adding ingredients.

SELECTING THE COOKING MODE

The Ninja Foodi offers a range of cooking modes, including pressure cook, air crisp, steam, bake/roast, and more. Press the mode selection button that corresponds to your desired cooking method. The digital display should indicate the selected mode.

ADJUSTING TIME AND TEMPERATURE

Once you have chosen the cooking mode, you can customize the time and temperature settings. Use the time adjustment buttons to set the desired cooking duration. Similarly, use the temperature adjustment buttons to select the appropriate cooking temperature. Refer to your recipe or cooking guidelines to determine the ideal settings.

PREHEATING THE NINJA FOODI (IF APPLICABLE)

Depending on the cooking mode, the Ninja Foodi may require preheating. If preheating is necessary, press the start button to initiate the preheating process. The digital display will show the preheating progress, and an indicator light may illuminate. It is important to note that not all cooking modes require preheating.

ADDING INGREDIENTS AND STARTING THE COOKING PROCESS

Once the Ninja Foodi is preheated or if preheating is not required, it's time to add your ingredients. Open the lid carefully, place the ingredients into the cooking pot or air frying basket, and close the lid securely. Press the start button to begin the cooking process. The digital display will show the remaining cooking time, allowing you to monitor the progress.

Pausing or Adjusting Settings (if necessary)
In some situations, you may need to pause or adjust the cooking settings during the process. To pause the cooking, press the stop button. This will temporarily halt the cooking process without canceling it entirely. To adjust the time or temperature, press the appropriate adjustment buttons and then press start to resume cooking with the updated settings.

UTILIZING THE KEEP WARM FUNCTION

Once the cooking is complete, the Ninja Foodi offers a convenient keep warm function. If you are not ready to serve the food immediately, activate the keep warm function by pressing the corresponding button. This feature ensures that your meal stays warm and ready to serve until you are ready to enjoy it.

CLEANING AND MAINTENANCE

After using the Ninja Foodi, it is important to clean and maintain it properly. Always unplug the appliance and allow it to cool before cleaning. Remove the cooking pot, air frying basket, and any other removable parts and wash them with warm, soapy water.

Wipe the control panel and the exterior of the appliance with a damp cloth. Take care not to submerge the control panel in water.

EXPLORING ADVANCED FEATURES AND RECIPES

Once you have mastered the basic controls, you can delve into the advanced features and recipes that the Ninja Foodi offers. Experiment with different cooking modes, try out new recipes, and push the boundaries of your culinary creativity. The more you explore, the more you'll appreciate the versatility and potential of the Ninja Foodi.

Exploring the Multifunctionality of the Ninja Foodi

The Ninja Foodi is not your average kitchen appliance. It is a multifunctional powerhouse that combines several cooking methods into a single device, revolutionizing the way you prepare meals. In this in-depth exploration, we will delve into the various functions of the Ninja Foodi and discover the incredible culinary possibilities it offers.

PRESSURE COOKING

The Ninja Foodi's pressure cooking function is a game-changer for busy individuals seeking fast and flavorful meals. By harnessing the power of pressure, this cooking method significantly reduces cooking times while infusing food with rich flavors and tenderness. From soups and stews to braised meats and risottos, pressure cooking in the Ninja Foodi ensures consistent and delicious results.

AIR FRYING

With its air frying capabilities, the Ninja Foodi takes guilt-free indulgence to new heights. Air frying allows you to achieve that crispy,

golden-brown texture on your favorite foods using minimal oil. From crispy fries and crunchy chicken wings to vegetables and even desserts, the Foodi's air frying function provides a healthier alternative to deep-frying without compromising on taste.

ROASTING AND BAKING

The Ninja Foodi's roasting and baking functions open up a world of possibilities for culinary creativity. Whether you're roasting a succulent chicken, searing vegetables for a flavorful side dish, or baking a moist and decadent cake, the Foodi's precise temperature control and even heat distribution ensure consistent and delectable results every time.

GRILLING AND SEARING

Craving that distinct charred flavor and appetizing grill marks? The Ninja Foodi's grilling and searing functions allow you to enjoy grilled delicacies without stepping foot outdoors. From juicy steaks and tender kebabs to perfectly seared fish fillets, the Foodi's high heat capability brings the joy of grilling directly to your kitchen.

STEAMING

Steaming is a healthy and gentle cooking method that preserves the nutrients and flavors of your ingredients. The Ninja Foodi's steaming function offers an efficient and convenient way to prepare a variety of dishes, from steamed vegetables and dumplings to fish and even desserts like steamed puddings. With the Foodi, you can enjoy vibrant and nutritious meals in no time.

SLOW COOKING

The slow cooking function of the Ninja Foodi allows you to simmer and slow-cook your favorite recipes to perfection. Whether you're preparing tender braised meats, hearty stews, or comforting soups, the Foodi's low and slow cooking method ensures that flavors meld together and ingredients become fork-tender for a satisfying and comforting meal.

DEHYDRATING

With the Ninja Foodi's dehydrating function, you can transform fruits, vegetables, and herbs into flavorful and nutritious snacks. Whether you're making dried fruit chips, beef jerky, or homemade dried herbs for seasoning, the Foodi's low heat and air circulation create the ideal environment for preserving food while intensifying its natural flavors.

CUSTOMIZABLE COOKING

The Ninja Foodi's versatility doesn't end with its pre-set functions. It also offers customizable cooking options, allowing you to adjust time, temperature, and other parameters to suit your specific needs. This flexibility empowers you to experiment with different recipes, adapt cooking techniques, and unleash your culinary creativity with confidence.

RECIPE INSPIRATION

The Ninja Foodi comes with a wealth of recipe inspiration to help you get started and explore its multifunctionality. From online resources to dedicated cookbooks, you'll find an abundance of recipes tailored to the Ninja Foodi's capabilities. Experiment with new flavors, try diverse cuisines, and discover dishes you never thought possible—all with the guidance of tried-and-tested recipes.

TIME AND SPACE SAVINGS

Perhaps one of the most significant advantages of the Ninja Foodi's multifunctionality is the time and space it saves in the kitchen. By combining multiple cooking methods into one device, you can streamline your cooking process, reduce the number of appliances cluttering your countertop, and spend less time on cleaning and maintenance.

Troubleshooting Your Ninja Foodi

COMMON ISSUES AND SOLUTIONS FOR BEGINNERS

The Ninja Foodi is a versatile and innovative kitchen appliance that can greatly enhance your cooking experience. However, like any appliance, beginners may encounter some common issues while using it. In this guide, we will address these issues and provide simple solutions to help you overcome them.

ISSUE: FOOD NOT COOKING EVENLY

Solution: Uneven cooking can occur if the food is overcrowded or if the cooking pot or air frying basket is not properly arranged. Ensure that you leave enough space between ingredients for proper air circulation. Consider cooking in smaller batches if needed. Also, make sure the food is evenly distributed in the cooking pot or air frying basket to promote even cooking.

ISSUE: FOOD STICKING TO THE COOKING POT OR AIR FRYING BASKET

Solution: To prevent food from sticking, ensure that the cooking pot or air frying basket is properly greased or lined with parchment paper, as recommended in the recipe. Additionally, avoid overcrowding the cooking pot or air frying basket, as this can lead to increased moisture and potential sticking.

ISSUE: EXCESSIVE SMOKE OR ODOR DURING AIR FRYING

Solution: Excessive smoke or odor may occur if there is too much oil or grease on the food. Make sure to follow the recommended amount of oil or use a cooking spray for air frying. Additionally, clean the air frying basket and remove any excess oil or residue that could cause smoke or odor.

ISSUE: LID NOT SEALING PROPERLY

Solution: If the lid of the Ninja Foodi is not sealing properly, it can affect the cooking process. Ensure that the silicone gasket on the lid is clean and properly inserted. Also, make sure there are no food particles or debris obstructing the sealing mechanism. Adjust the lid carefully and ensure that it is firmly in place before starting the cooking process.

ISSUE: DIFFICULTY IN PROGRAMMING THE CONTROL PANEL

Solution: Programming the control panel may be challenging for beginners. Refer to the user manual or recipe instructions for step-by-step guidance on setting the cooking mode, time, and temperature. Take your time to familiarize yourself with the control panel layout and practice programming it. With practice, you will become more comfortable

and proficient in using the controls.

ISSUE: OVERCOOKING OR UNDER-COOKING FOOD

Solution: Achieving the desired level of doneness can take some trial and error, especially with new recipes or unfamiliar ingredients. Follow the recommended cooking times and temperatures in recipes as a starting point. Use a food thermometer to ensure that meats and other ingredients are cooked to the appropriate internal temperature. Adjust the cooking time and temperature as needed based on your preferences and results.

ISSUE: DIFFICULTY IN CLEANING THE NINJA FOODI

Solution: Cleaning the Ninja Foodi is essential for proper maintenance. Ensure that the appliance is unplugged and cooled before cleaning. Remove any removable parts, such as the cooking pot and air frying basket, and wash them with warm, soapy water. Wipe the control panel and the exterior of the appliance with a damp cloth. Take care not to submerge the control panel in water. Refer to the user manual for specific cleaning instructions.

ISSUE: ERROR MESSAGES OR MALFUNCTIONS

Solution: If you encounter error messages or experience malfunctions with your Ninja Foodi, consult the user manual or contact customer support for assistance. Error messages can provide valuable information about the issue, and customer support can guide you through troubleshooting steps or arrange for repairs if necessary.

In conclusion, the Ninja Foodi is a remarkable kitchen appliance that offers a wide range of cooking functions and possibilities. While beginners may encounter some common issues, such as uneven cooking, food sticking, or difficulty in programming the control panel, these challenges can be easily overcome with a little knowledge and practice. By following the provided solutions and tips, you can navigate these obstacles and unlock the full potential of the Ninja Foodi. Embrace the versatility, experiment with recipes, and enjoy the convenience and delicious results that this multifunctional appliance brings to your culinary adventures. Get ready to elevate your cooking skills and embark on a delightful culinary journey with the Ninja Foodi.

Chapter 2

Breakfast Recipes

Baked Breakfast Quiche

Prep time: 5 minutes | Cook time: 55 minutes
|Serves 6

- 8 eggs
- 1 cup sour cream
- 3/4 tbsp ranch seasoning
- 1 1/2 cups cheddar cheese, shredded
- 1 lb ground Italian sausage
- Pepper
- Salt

1. Brown the ground sausage in a pan over medium heat. Drain well and set aside.
2. In a large bowl, whisk eggs with cream, ranch seasoning, pepper, and salt. Add sausage and cheese and stir well.
3. Pour egg mixture into the greased baking dish.
4. Select bake mode then set the temperature to 350 F and time for 55 minutes. Press start.
5. Once the oven is preheated then place the baking dish into the oven.
6. Slice and serve.

Hash Brown Egg Cups

Prep time: 5 minutes | Cook time: 30 minutes
|Serves 12

- 8 eggs
- 2 tbsp milk
- 1/4 tsp garlic powder
- 1 cup ham, cubed
- 1 1/2 cups cheddar cheese, grated
- 20 oz hash browns
- Pepper
- Salt

1. Spray 12-cups muffin pan with cooking spray and set aside.
2. In a bowl, whisk eggs with milk, pepper, and salt. Add ham, cheese, and hash browns and stir to combine.
3. Pour egg mixture into the greased muffin pan.
4. Select bake then set the temperature to 350 F and time to 30 minutes. Press start.
5. Once the oven is preheated then place the muffin pan into the oven.
6. Serve and enjoy.

Spicy Egg Casserole

Prep time: 5 minutes | Cook time: 25 minutes
|Serves 8

- 8 eggs
- 1/2 cup milk
- 2 tbsp flour
- 6.5 oz can green chiles, chopped
- 8 oz cheddar cheese, grated
- 6 oz Monterey jack cheese, grated
- Pepper
- Salt

1. In a bowl, mix cheddar cheese and Monterey jack cheese then sprinkle 1 cup cheese in a greased baking dish.
2. Pour green chilies over cheese.
3. In a bowl, whisk eggs with milk, flour, pepper, and salt.
4. Pour egg mixture over green chilies.
5. Select bake mode then set the temperature to 350 F and time for 25 minutes. Press start.
6. Once the oven is preheated then place the baking dish into the oven.
7. Slice and serve.

Potato & Corned Beef Casserole

Prep time: 5 minutes | Cook time: 1 hour 20 minutes |Serves 3

- 3 Yukon Gold potatoes
- 2 tablespoons unsalted butter
- ½ of onion, chopped
- 2 garlic cloves, minced
- 2 tablespoons vegetable oil
- ½ teaspoon salt
- 12 ounces corned beef
- 3 eggs

1. Press AIR OVEN MODE button of Ninja Foodi Dual Heat Air Fry Oven and turn the dial to select "Bake" mode.
2. Press TIME/SLICES button and again turn the dial to set the cooking time to 30 minutes.
3. Now push TEMP/SHADE button and rotate the dial to set the temperature at 350 degrees F.
4. Press "Start/Stop" button to start.
5. When the unit beeps to show that it is preheated, open the oven door and grease the air fry basket.
6. Place the potatoes into the prepared air fry basket and insert in the oven.
7. When cooking time is completed, open the oven door and transfer the potatoes onto a tray.
8. Set aside to cool for about 15 minutes.
9. After cooling, cut the potatoes into ½-inch-thick slices.
10. In a skillet, melt the butter over medium heat and cook the onion and garlic for about 10 minutes.
11. Remove from the heat and place the onion mixture into a casserole dish.
12. Add the potato slices, oil, salt, and corned beef and mix well.
13. Press AIR OVEN MODE button of Ninja Foodi Dual Heat Air Fry Oven and turn the dial to select "Bake" mode.
14. Press TIME/SLICES button and again turn the dial to set the cooking time to 40 minutes.
15. Now push TEMP/SHADE button and rotate the dial to set the temperature at 350 degrees F.
16. Press "Start/Stop" button to start.
17. When the unit beeps to show that it is preheated, open the oven door.
18. Arrange the casserole dish over the wire rack and insert in the oven.
19. After 30 minutes of cooking, remove the casserole dish and crack 3 eggs on top.
20. When cooking time is completed, open the oven door and serve immediately.

Butternut Breakfast Squash

Prep time: 10 minutes | Cook time: 15 minutes | Serves 4

- 1 tbsp. coconut oil
- 12 oz. butternut squash, cubed
- 1 tbsp. peanut butter
- ¼ tsp cinnamon
- ¼ tsp all-spice
- 2 tsp maple syrup

1. Select sauté function on medium heat and add the coconut oil to the cooking pot.
2. Add the squash and cook until it starts to soften, about 8-10 minutes.
3. Add remaining ingredients and mix well. Cook 2-3 minutes longer until heated through. Serve warm.

Basic Breakfast Bread

Prep time: 5 minutes | Cook time: 15 minutes |Serves 4

- ⅞ cup whole-wheat flour
- ⅞ cup plain flour
- 1 ¾ ounces pumpkin seeds
- 1 teaspoon salt
- ½ of sachet instant yeast
- ½-1 cup lukewarm water

1. In a bowl, mix the flours, pumpkin seeds, salt, and yeast and mix well.
2. Slowly, add the desired amount of water and mix until a soft dough ball forms. With your hands, knead the dough until smooth and elastic.
3. Place the dough ball into a bowl. With plastic wrap, cover the bowl and set it aside in a warm place for 30 minutes or until doubled in size.
4. Press the START/PAUSE button and turn on your Ninja Foodi Digital Air Fry Oven and set temperatures to 350 degrees F for 18 minutes on the "AIR CRISP" function.
5. Press the "START/PAUSE" button to start. Place the dough ball in a greased cake pan and brush the top of the dough with water.
6. When the unit beeps to show that it is preheated, open the door. Place the cake pan into the Air Crisp Basket and insert it in the oven.
7. When cooking time is completed, open the door and place the pan onto a wire rack for about 10-15 minutes.
8. Carefully invert the bread onto the wire rack to cool completely cool before slicing.
9. Cut the bread into desired-sized slices and serve.

Blueberry-lemon Scones

Prep time: 5 minutes | Cook time: 25 minutes |Serves 6

- 2 cups all-purpose flour
- 1 tablespoon baking powder
- 2 teaspoons sugar
- 1 teaspoon kosher salt
- 2 ounces refined coconut oil
- 1 cup fresh blueberries
- ¼ ounce lemon zest
- 8 ounces coconut milk

1. Blend coconut oil with salt, sugar, baking powder, and flour in a food processor.
2. Transfer this flour mixture to a mixing bowl.
3. Now add coconut milk and lemon zest to the flour mixture, then mix well.
4. Fold in blueberries and mix the prepared dough well until smooth.
5. Spread this blueberry dough into a 7-inch round and place it in a pan.
6. Refrigerate the blueberry dough for 15 minutes, then slice it into 6 wedges.
7. Layer the SearPlate with a parchment sheet.
8. Place the blueberry wedges in the lined SearPlate.
9. Transfer the scones to Ninja Foodi Dual Heat Air Fry Oven and close the door.
10. Select "Bake" mode by rotating the dial.
11. Press the TIME/SLICES button and change the value to 25 minutes.
12. Press the TEMP/SHADE button and change the value to 400 degrees F.
13. Press Start/Stop to begin cooking.
14. Serve fresh.

Breakfast Souffles

Prep time: 15 minutes | Cook time: 20 minutes | Serves 6

- 1 lb. thick cut bacon, chopped
- 8 oz. pork sausage links, chopped
- nonstick cooking spray
- 5 eggs, separated
- 1/3 cup heavy cream
- ½ cup cheddar cheese, grated
- ½ tsp salt
- ¼ tsp thyme

1. Set cooker to sauté function on med-high.
2. Add the bacon and cook until almost crisp. Transfer to a paper towel lined plate.
3. Add the sausage and cook until done. Transfer to a separate paper towel lined plate.
4. Drain off fat and set cooker to air fry setting. Preheat to 350°F.
5. Spray 6 ramekins with cooking spray.
6. In a large bowl, beat egg whites until stiff peaks form.
7. In a medium bowl, whisk the yolks, cream, cheese, and seasonings together. Stir in the meats and mix well.
8. Gently fold the yolk mixture into the egg whites. Spoon the mixture into the prepared ramekins.
9. Place the rack in the cooker and place the ramekins on top. Secure the tender-crisp lid and bake 20 minutes, or until the soufflés have puffed up. Serve immediately.

Apple Walnut Quinoa

Prep time: 5 minutes | Cook time: 15 minutes | Serves 2

- ½ cup quinoa, rinsed
- 1 apple, cored & chopped
- 2 cups water
- ½ cup apple juice, unsweetened
- 2 tsp maple syrup
- 1 tsp cinnamon
- ¼ cup walnuts, chopped & lightly toasted

1. Set the cooker to sauté on med-low heat. Add the quinoa and apples and cook, stirring frequently, 5 minutes.
2. Add water and apple juice and stir to mix. Secure the lid and set to pressure cooking on high. Set timer for 10 minutes.
3. When timer goes off use quick release to remove the lid. Quinoa should be tender and the liquid should be absorbed, if not cook another 5 minutes.
4. When quinoa is done, stir in syrup and cinnamon. Sprinkle nuts over top and serve.

Cinnamon Sugar French Toast Bites

Prep time: 10 minutes | Cook time: 10 minutes | Serves 4

- butter flavored cooking spray
- 1/3 cup Stevia
- 1 tsp cinnamon
- 4 slices sourdough bread, sliced thick, remove crust
- 2 eggs
- 2 tbsp. milk
- 1 tsp vanilla

1. Set to air fryer function on 350°F. Spray the fryer basket with cooking spray.
2. In a medium bowl, whisk together eggs, milk, and vanilla until smooth.
3. Slice bread into bite-size cubes, about 8 pieces per slice. Dip in egg mixture to coat. Place in a single layer in the fryer basket and spray lightly with cooking spray.
4. Secure the tender-crisp lid and cook 3-5 minutes until golden brown, turning over halfway through cooking time.
5. Roll French toast bites in cinnamon mixture and serve. Repeat with remaining bread and egg mixture.

Breakfast Burrito Bake

Prep time: 10 minutes | Cook time: 40 minutes | Serves 8

- 14 oz. pinto beans, drain & rinse
- 2 cups mild salsa
- 2 cups baby spinach, chopped
- 1 tsp cumin
- 1 tsp oregano
- nonstick cooking spray
- 8 corn tortillas, gluten-free
- 1 ½ cups sharp cheddar cheese, grated
- 6 eggs
- ½ cup skim milk

1. In a large bowl, combine the beans, salsa, spinach, cumin and oregano.
2. Spray an 8-inch baking dish with cooking spray.
3. Spread ¼ cup bean mixture in the bottom of the dish. Top with 4 tortillas, overlapping as necessary.
4. Top tortillas with half the remaining bean mixture and sprinkle with half the cheese.
5. On top of the cheese lay the remaining tortillas and cover with remaining bean mixture.
6. In a medium bowl, whisk together eggs and milk. Pour over casserole. Cover and refrigerate overnight.
7. Place the baking dish in the cooking pot and add the tender-crisp lid. Select air fryer function on 350°F. Bake 25-30 minutes, or until eggs are set and top starts to brown.
8. Sprinkle remaining cheese over the top and bake another 5 minutes until cheese melts. Let cool slightly before cutting and serving.

Pumpkin Coconut Breakfast Bake

Prep time: **10 minutes** | Cook time: **1 hour 15 minutes** | **Serves 8**

- butter flavored cooking spray
- 5 eggs
- ½ cup coconut milk
- 2 cups pumpkin puree
- 1 banana, mashed
- 2 dates, pitted & chopped
- 1 tsp cinnamon
- 1 cup raspberries
- ¼ cup coconut, unsweetened & shredded

1. Lightly spray an 8-inch baking dish with cooking spray.
2. In a large bowl, whisk together eggs and milk.
3. Whisk in pumpkin until combined.
4. Sprinkle berries over top.
5. Place the rack in the cooking pot and place the dish on it. Add the tender-crisp lid and select bake on 350°F. Bake 20 minutes.
6. Sprinkle coconut over the top and bake another 20-25 minutes until top is lightly browned and casserole is set. Slice and serve warm.

Lush Vegetable Frittata

Prep time: **15 minutes** | Cook time: **21 minutes** | **Serves 2**

- 4 eggs
- ¼ cup milk
- Sea salt and ground black pepper, to taste
- 1 zucchini, sliced
- ½ bunch asparagus, sliced
- ½ cup mushrooms, sliced
- ½ cup spinach, shredded
- ½ cup red onion, sliced
- ½ tablespoon olive oil
- 5 tablespoons feta cheese, crumbled
- 4 tablespoons Cheddar cheese, grated
- ¼ bunch chives, minced

1. In a bowl, mix the eggs, milk, salt and pepper.
2. Over a medium heat, sauté the vegetables for 6 minutes with the olive oil in a nonstick pan.
3. Select the BAKE function and preheat Ninja Foodi to 320°F (160°C).
4. Transfer the baking tin to the air fryer oven and bake for 15 minutes. Remove the frittata from the air fryer oven and leave to cool for 5 minutes.
5. Top with the minced chives and serve.

Cheddar Bacon Quiche

Prep time: **15 minutes** | Cook time: **20 minutes** | **Serves 4**

- 1 tablespoon olive oil
- 1 shortcrust pastry
- 3 tablespoons Greek yogurt
- ½ cup grated Cheddar cheese
- 3 ounces (85 g) chopped bacon
- 4 eggs, beaten
- ¼ teaspoon onion powder
- ¼ teaspoon sea salt
- Flour, for sprinkling

1. Select the BAKE function and preheat Ninja Foodi to 330°F (166°C).
2. Take 8 ramekins and grease with olive oil. Coat with a sprinkling of flour, tapping to remove any excess.
3. Cut the shortcrust pastry in 8 and place each piece at the bottom of each ramekin.
4. Put all the other ingredients in a bowl and combine well. Spoon equal amounts of the filling into each piece of pastry.
5. Bake the ramekins in the air fryer oven for 20 minutes.
6. Serve warm.

Curried Chicken and Mushroom Casserole

Prep time: 15 minutes | Cook time: 20 minutes | Serves 4

- 4 chicken breasts
- 1 tablespoon curry powder
- 1 cup coconut milk
- Salt, to taste
- 1 broccoli, cut into florets
- 1 cup mushrooms
- ½ cup shredded Parmesan cheese
- Cooking spray

1. Select the BAKE function and preheat Ninja Foodi to 350°F (177°C). Spritz a casserole dish with cooking spray.
2. Cube the chicken breasts and combine with curry powder and coconut milk in a bowl. Season with salt.
3. Add the broccoli and mushroom and mix well.
4. Pour the mixture into the casserole dish. Top with the cheese.
5. Transfer to the air fryer oven and bake for about 20 minutes.
6. Serve warm.

Double Chocolate Quinoa Bowl

Prep time: 5 minutes | Cook time: 15 minutes | Serves 2

- ½ cup quinoa
- 1 cup water
- 1 cup coconut milk
- 2 tsp honey
- 2 tsp chia seeds
- 2 tsp cocoa powder
- 1 oz. dark chocolate, chopped
- 1 tbsp. pecans, chopped
- 1 tbsp. coconut flakes

1. Place quinoa and water in the cooking pot, stir.
2. Add the lid and select pressure cooker on high. Set timer for 10 minutes. When timer goes off, use quick release to remove the lid.
3. Set to sauté on med-low. Cook, stirring until all liquid is absorbed.
4. Stir in milk, honey, chia seeds, and cocoa powder. Cook, stirring, until heated through.
5. Ladle into bowls and top with chocolate, nuts, and coconut. Serve warm.

Creamy-Cheesy Tomato Casserole

Prep time: 5 minutes | Cook time: 30 minutes | Serves 4

- 5 eggs
- 2 tablespoons heavy cream
- 3 tablespoons chunky tomato sauce
- 2 tablespoons grated Parmesan cheese, plus more for topping

1. Select the BAKE function and preheat Ninja Foodi to 350°F (177°C).
1. Combine the eggs and cream in a bowl.
2. Mix in the tomato sauce and add the cheese.
3. Spread into a glass baking dish and bake in the preheated air fryer oven for 30 minutes.
4. Top with extra cheese and serve.

Chapter 3

Snacks & Appetizer Recipes

Tofu Nuggets

Prep time: 5 minutes | Cook time: 30 minutes
|Serves 4

- 1 lb firm tofu, cut into cubes
- 1/2 tsp paprika
- 1 tsp Italian seasoning
- 1/2 tsp garlic powder
- 1 tsp onion powder
- 1/4 cup rice flour
- 1/4 cup Nutritional yeast flakes
- 1 tbsp liquid aminos
- 1 tsp salt

1. Add tofu and liquid aminos into the mixing bowl. Mix well and let it marinate for 20 minutes.
2. Spray sheet pan with cooking spray.
3. Select bake mode then set the temperature to 400 F and time for 30 minutes. Press start.
4. Once the oven is preheated then place the sheet pan into the oven.
5. Turn tofu pieces halfway through.
6. Serve and enjoy.

Baked Mozzarella Sticks

Prep time: 5 minutes | Cook time: 8 minutes
|Serves 6

- ½ cup Italian Style bread crumbs
- ¾ cup panko break crumbs
- ¼ cup parmesan cheese
- 1 tablespoon garlic powder
- 12 mozzarella cheese sticks
- Cooking spray

1. Make mozzarella sticks by freezing them for an hour or two. Take the mozzarella sticks out of the fridge and cut them in half so that each one is 2-3 inches long.
2. Combine the Panko, Italian Style bread crumbs, parmesan cheese, and garlic

powder on a dish and stir well.
3. Whisk together the eggs in a separate bowl.
4. On a nonstick pan, arrange mozzarella sticks in a single layer.
5. Freeze for an hour and take the mozzarella sticks out of the freezer and dip them in the egg and breadcrumb mixture once more.
6. Using cooking spray, lightly coat the SearPlate. Place the cheese sticks.
7. Turn on Ninja Foodi Dual Heat Air Fry Oven and rotate the knob to select "Bake".
8. Select the timer for 10 minutes and the temperature for 360 degrees F.
9. Remove and serve.

Tuna Breakfast Muffins

Prep time: 5 minutes | Cook time: 25 minutes
|Serves 8

- 2 eggs, lightly beaten
- 1/4 cup sour cream
- 1/4 cup mayonnaise
- 1 tsp cayenne
- 1 celery stalk, chopped
- 1 1/2 cups mozzarella cheese, shredded
- Pepper
- Salt

1. Place rack in the bottom position and close door. Select bake mode set the temperature to 350 F and set the timer to 25 minutes. Press the setting dial to preheat.
2. In a bowl, whisk eggs with pepper and salt. Add remaining ingredients and stir well.
3. Pour egg mixture into the greased muffin pan.
4. Once the unit is preheated, open the door, and place the muffin pan onto the center of the rack, and close the door.

Glazed Chicken Wings

Prep time: 5 minutes | Cook time: 25 minutes |Serves 4

- 1½ pounds chicken wingettes and drumettes
- ⅓ cup tomato sauce
- 2 tablespoons balsamic vinegar
- 2 tablespoons maple syrup
- ½ teaspoon liquid smoke
- ¼ teaspoon red pepper flakes, crushed
- Salt, as required

1. Arrange the wings onto the greased SearPlate.
2. Press AIR OVEN MODE button of Ninja Foodi Dual Heat Air Fry Oven and turn the dial to select "Air Fry" mode.
3. Press TIME/SLICES button and again turn the dial to set the cooking time to 25 minutes.
4. Now push TEMP/SHADE button and rotate the dial to set the temperature at 380 degrees F.
5. Press "Start/Stop" button to start.
6. When the unit beeps to show that it is preheated, open the oven door and insert the SearPlate in oven.
7. Meanwhile, in a small pan, add the remaining ingredients over medium heat and cook for about 10 minutes, stirring occasionally.
8. When cooking time is completed, open the oven door and place the chicken wings into a bowl.
9. Add the sauce and toss to coat well.
10. Serve immediately.

Ham & Egg Cups

Prep time: 5 minutes | Cook time: 18 minutes |Serves 6

- 6 ham slices
- 6 eggs
- 6 tablespoons cream
- 3 tablespoons mozzarella cheese, shredded
- ¼ teaspoon dried basil, crushed

1. Lightly grease 6 cups of a silicone muffin tin.
2. Line each prepared muffin cup with 1 ham slice.
3. Crack 1 egg into each muffin cup and top with cream.
4. Sprinkle with cheese and basil.
5. Press AIR OVEN MODE button of Ninja Foodi Dual Heat Air Fry Oven and turn the dial to select "Air Fry" mode.
6. Press TIME/SLICES button and again turn the dial to set the cooking time to 18 minutes.
7. Now push TEMP/SHADE button and rotate the dial to set the temperature at 350 degrees F.
8. Press "Start/Stop" button to start.
9. When the unit beeps to show that it is preheated, open the oven door.
10. Arrange the muffin tin over the wire rack and insert in the oven.
11. When cooking time is completed, open the oven door and place the muffin tin onto a wire rack to cool for about 5 minutes.
12. Carefully invert the muffins onto the platter and serve warm.

Buttermilk Biscuits

Prep time: 5 minutes | Cook time: 8 minutes |Serves 8

- ½ cup cake flour
- ¼ teaspoon baking soda
- ½ teaspoon baking powder
- 1 teaspoon granulated sugar
- Salt, to taste
- ¼ cup cold unsalted butter, cut into cubes
- ¾ cup buttermilk
- 2 tablespoons butter, melted

1. In a large bowl, sift together flours, baking soda, baking powder, sugar, and salt.
2. With a pastry cutter, cut cold butter and mix until coarse crumb forms.
3. Slowly, add buttermilk and mix until a smooth dough forms.
4. Place the dough onto a floured surface and with your hands, press it into ½-inch thickness.
5. With a 1¾-inch-round cookie cutter, cut the biscuits.
6. Arrange the biscuits into SearPlate in a single layer and coat with the butter.
7. Press AIR OVEN MODE button of Ninja Foodi Dual Heat Air Fry Oven and turn the dial to select "Air Fry" mode.
8. Press TIME/SLICES button and again turn the dial to set the cooking time to 8 minutes.
9. Now push TEMP/SHADE button and rotate the dial to set the temperature at 400 degrees F.
10. Press "Start/Stop" button to start.
11. When the unit beeps to show that it is preheated, open the oven door.
12. Insert the SearPlate in the oven.
13. When cooking time is completed, open the oven door and place the SearPlate onto a wire rack for about 5 minutes.
14. Carefully invert the biscuits onto the wire rack to cool completely before serving.

Crispy Lemon-Pepper Wings

Prep Time: 5 Minutes | Cooking Time: 24 Minutes | Serves 10

- 2 pounds chicken wing flats and drumettes (about 16 to 20 pieces)
- 1½ teaspoons kosher salt or ¾ teaspoon fine salt
- 1½ teaspoons baking powder
- 4½ teaspoons salt-free lemon pepper seasoning (I use Penzey's Sunny Spain mix)
- Place the wings in a large bowl.

1. In a small bowl, stir together the salt, baking powder, and seasoning mix. Sprinkle the mixture over the wings and toss thoroughly to coat the wings. (This works best with your hands.) If you have time, let the wings sit for 20 to 30 minutes. Place the wings on the sheet pan, making sure they don't crowd each other too much.
2. Select AIR FRY, set temperature to 375°F, and set time to 24 minutes. Select START/PAUSE to begin preheating.
3. Once preheated, slide the pan into the oven.
4. After 12 minutes, remove the pan from the oven. Using tongs, turn the wings over. Rotate the pan 180 degrees and return the pan to the oven to continue cooking.
5. When cooking is complete, the wings should be dark golden brown and a bit charred in places. Remove the pan from the oven and let cool for before serving.

Savory Sausage Rolls

Prep Time: 15 Minutes | Cooking Time: 15 Minutes | Serves 12

- 1 pound bulk breakfast sausage
- ½ cup finely chopped onion (about ½ medium onion)
- 1 garlic clove, minced or pressed
- ½ teaspoon dried sage (optional)
- ¼ teaspoon cayenne pepper
- ½ teaspoon dried mustard
- 1 large egg, beaten lightly
- ½ cup fresh bread crumbs
- 2 sheets (1 package) frozen puff pastry, thawed
- All-purpose flour, for dusting

1. In a medium bowl, break up the sausage. Add the onion, garlic, sage (if using), cayenne, mustard, egg, and bread crumbs. Mix to combine. Divide the sausage mixture in half and tightly wrap each half in plastic wrap. Refrigerate for 5 to 10 minutes.
2. Lay out one of the pastry sheets on a lightly floured cutting board. Using a rolling pin, lightly roll out the pastry to smooth out the dough. Take out one of the sausage packages and form the sausage into a long roll (it's easiest to do this while the sausage is in the plastic wrap). Remove the plastic wrap and place the sausage on top of the puff pastry about 1 inch from one of the long edges. Roll the pastry around the sausage and pinch the edges of the dough together to seal. Repeat with the other pastry sheet and sausage. Slice the logs into lengths about 1½ inches long. (If you have the time, freeze the logs for 10 minutes or so before slicing| it's much easier to slice.) Place the sausage rolls on the sheet pan, cut-side down.
3. Select AIR ROAST, set temperature to 350°F, and set time to 15 minutes. Select START/PAUSE to begin preheating.
4. Once the unit has preheated, slide the pan into the oven.
5. After 7 or 8 minutes, rotate the pan 180 degrees and continue cooking.
6. When cooking is complete, the rolls will be golden brown and sizzling. Remove the pan from the oven and let cool for 5 minutes or so. If you like, serve them with honey mustard for dipping.

Potato Chips

Prep time: 5 minutes | Cook time: 25 minutes |Serves 2

- 1 medium Russet potato, sliced
- 1 tablespoon canola oil
- ¼ teaspoon sea salt
- ¼ teaspoon black pepper
- 1 teaspoon chopped fresh rosemary

1. Fill a suitable glass bowl with cold water and add sliced potatoes.
2. Leave the potatoes for 20 minutes, then drain them. Pat dry the chips with a paper towel.
3. Toss the potatoes with salt, black pepper, and oil to coat well.
4. Spread the potato slices in the air fry basket evenly.
5. Transfer the basket to Ninja Foodi Dual Heat Air Fry Oven and close the door.
6. Select "Air Fry" mode by rotating the dial.
7. Press the TIME/SLICES button and change the value to 25 minutes.
8. Press the TEMP/SHADE button and change the value to 375 degrees F.
9. Press Start/Stop to begin cooking.
10. Garnish with rosemary.
11. Serve warm.

Pepperoni Pizza Bites

Prep Time: 12 Minutes | Cooking Time: 16 Minutes | Serves 8

- ½ cup (2 ounces) pepperoni (very finely chopped)
- 1 cup finely shredded mozzarella cheese
- ¼ cup Marinara Sauce or store-bought variety
- 1 (8-ounce) can crescent roll dough
- All-purpose flour, for dusting

1. In a small bowl, toss together the pepperoni and cheese. Stir in the marinara sauce. (If you have one, this is a good time to use a food processor. Then you don't have to chop everything so fine| just dump everything in and pulse a few times to mix.)
2. Unroll the dough onto a lightly floured cutting board. Separate it into 4 rectangles. Firmly pinch the perforations together and pat or roll the dough pieces flat.
3. Divide the cheese mixture evenly between the rectangles and spread it out over the dough, leaving a ¼-inch border. Roll a rectangle up tightly, starting with the short end. Pinch the edge down to seal the roll. Repeat with the remaining rolls. If you have time, refrigerate or freeze the rolls for 5 to 10 minutes to firm up. This makes slicing easier.
4. Slice the rolls into 4 or 5 even slices. Place the slices on the sheet pan, leaving a few inches between each.
5. Select AIR ROAST, set temperature to 350°F, and set time to 12 minutes. Select START/PAUSE to begin preheating.
6. Once the unit has preheated, slide the pan into the oven.
7. After 6 minutes, rotate the pan 180 degrees and continue cooking.
8. When cooking is complete, the rolls will be golden brown with crisp edges. Remove the pan from the oven. If you like, serve with additional marinara sauce for dipping.

Carrot Chips

Prep time: 5 minutes | Cook time: 15 minutes |Serves 8

- 2 pounds carrots, sliced
- ¼ cup olive oil
- 1 tablespoon sea salt
- 1 teaspoon ground cumin
- 1 teaspoon ground cinnamon

1. Toss the carrot slices with oil, sea salt, cumin, and cinnamon in a large bowl.
2. Grease the SearPlate and spread the carrot slices in it.
3. Transfer the SearPlate to Ninja Foodi Dual Heat Air Fry Oven and close the door.
4. Select "Bake" mode by rotating the dial.
5. Press the TIME/SLICES button and change the value to 15 minutes.
6. Press the TEMP/SHADE button and change the value to 450 degrees F.
7. Press Start/Stop to begin cooking.
8. Flip the chips after 7-8 minutes of cooking and resume baking.
9. Serve fresh.

Butternut Squash

Prep time: 5 minutes | Cook time: 20 minutes |Serves 4

- 4 cups butternut squash, cubed
- 1 teaspoon cinnamon
- Olive oil cooking spray

1. Spray the air fry basket or line it with foil and spray it with olive oil cooking spray.
2. Place the butternut squash in the basket.
3. Coat with olive oil and sprinkle with cinnamon.
4. Place inside the oven.
5. Turn on Ninja Foodi Dual Heat Air Fry Oven and rotate the knob to select "Bake".
6. Select the timer for 20 minutes and the temperature for 390 degrees F.
7. Serve immediately after cooking.

Pimento Cheese-Stuffed Mushrooms

Prep Time: 15 Minutes | Cooking Time: 12 Minutes | Serves 12

- 24 medium raw white button or cremini mushrooms (about 1½ inches in diameter)
- 4 ounces shredded extra-sharp cheddar cheese
- 2 tablespoons grated onion
- 1 ounce chopped jarred pimientos or roasted red pepper (about ¼ cup)
- ⅛ teaspoon smoked paprika
- ⅛ teaspoon hot sauce, such as Crystal or Tabasco
- 2 ounces cream cheese, at room temperature
- 2 tablespoons butter, melted, divided
- 2 tablespoons grated Parmesan cheese
- ⅓ cup panko bread crumbs

1. Wash the mushrooms and drain. Gently pull out the stems and discard (or save for another use| they make great vegetable stock). If your mushrooms are on the small side, or you feel like some extra work, you can use a small spoon or melon baller to remove some of the gills to form a larger cavity. Set aside.
2. In a medium bowl, combine the cheddar cheese, onion, pimientos, paprika, hot sauce, and cream cheese. The mixture should be smooth with no large streaks of cream cheese visible.
3. Brush the sheet pan with 1 tablespoon of melted butter. Arrange the mushrooms evenly over the pan, hollow-side up.
4. Place the cheese mixture into a large heavy plastic bag and cut off the end. Fill the mushrooms with the cheese mixture.
5. In a small bowl, stir together the Parmesan, panko, and remaining 1 tablespoon of melted butter. Sprinkle a little of the panko mixture over each mushroom (or carefully dip the filled tops of the mushrooms into the mixture to coat).
6. Select AIR ROAST, set temperature to 350°F, and set time to 18 minutes. Select START/PAUSE to begin preheating.
7. Once the unit has preheated, slide the pan into the oven.
8. After about 9 minutes, rotate the pan 180 degrees and continue cooking.
9. When cooking is complete, let the stuffed mushrooms cool slightly before serving.

Chapter 4

Beef, Pork & Lamb Recipes

Baked Pork Ribs

Prep time: 5 minutes | Cook time: 30 minutes |Serves 8

- 2 lbs pork ribs, boneless
- 1 ½ tablespoon garlic powder
- 1 tablespoon onion powder
- Salt and pepper to taste

1. Place pork ribs on a sheet pan and season with onion powder, garlic powder, pepper, and salt.
2. Place the wire rack inside.
3. Select "BAKE" mode, set the temperature to 350 degrees F, and set the time to 30 minutes.
4. Press "START/PAUSE" to begin preheating.
5. Once the oven is preheated, place the sheet pan on a wire rack and close the oven door to start cooking.
6. Cook for 30 minutes.
7. Serve and enjoy.

Glazed Lamb Chops

Prep time: 5 minutes | Cook time: 15 minutes |Serves 4

- 1 tablespoon Dijon mustard
- ½ tablespoon fresh lime juice
- 1 teaspoon honey
- ½ teaspoon olive oil
- Salt and black pepper, to taste
- 4 lamb loin chops

1. Mix the mustard, black pepper, lemon juice, oil, honey, salt, and black pepper in a bowl.
2. Add the chops and coat with the mixture generously.
3. Place the chops onto the greased sheet pan.
4. Insert the sheet pan in oven. Flip the chops once halfway through.

5. Select "BAKE" mode.
6. Press the "Time" button and turn the dial to set the cooking time to 15 minutes.
7. Now push the "Temp" button and rotate the dial to set the temperature at 390 degrees F.
8. Press the "START/PAUSE" button to start.
9. When the unit beeps to show that cooking time is completed, press the "Power" button to stop cooking and open the door.
10. Serve hot.

Steak Veggie Bites

Prep time: 5 minutes | Cook time: 8 minutes |Serves 2

- 1 lb ribeye steak, cut into cubes
- 2 cups broccoli florets
- 2 tbsp butter, melted
- 8 oz mushrooms, sliced
- 1 tbsp garlic, minced
- 1 tsp Worcestershire sauce
- Pepper
- Salt

1. Select air fry mode set the temperature to 400 F and set the timer to 8 minutes. Press the setting dial to preheat.
2. In a bowl, toss steak cubes with mushrooms, Worcestershire sauce, butter, broccoli, garlic, pepper, and salt.
3. Add steak and vegetable mixture into the air fryer basket.
4. Once the unit is preheated, open the door, and place the air fryer basket on the top level of the oven, and close the door.
5. Serve and enjoy.

Flavors Pork Chops

Prep time: 5 minutes | Cook time: 10 minutes |Serves 2

- 2 pork chops, boneless
- 1 tbsp canola oil
- 1/2 tsp lemon zest
- 1/2 tsp paprika
- 3/4 tsp rosemary, chopped
- 1/8 tsp red pepper flakes, crushed
- 1/4 tsp onion powder
- 1/4 tsp garlic powder
- Pepper
- Salt

1. Select air fry mode set the temperature to 390 F and set the timer to 10 minutes. Press the setting dial to preheat.
2. In a small bowl, mix rosemary, paprika, lemon zest, garlic powder, onion powder, red pepper flakes, pepper, and salt.
3. Brush pork chops with oil and rub with spice mixture.
4. Place pork chops into the air fryer basket.
5. Once the unit is preheated, open the door, and place the air fryer basket on the top level of the oven, and close the door.
6. Serve and enjoy.

Meatballs

Prep time: 5 minutes | Cook time: 8 minutes |Serves 6

- 1 egg
- 1 tsp Italian seasoning
- 4 oz ground pork
- 16 oz lean ground beef
- 1/3 cup Italian breadcrumbs
- 1/2 cup parmesan cheese, grated
- 1 tsp garlic, minced
- Pepper
Salt

1. Select air fry mode set the temperature to 350 F and set the timer to 8 minutes. Press the setting dial to preheat.
2. Add meat and remaining ingredients into the bowl and mix until well combined.
3. Make small balls from the meat mixture and place them into the air fryer basket.
4. Once the unit is preheated, open the door, and place the air fryer basket on the top level of the oven, and close the door.
5. Serve and enjoy.

Tarragon Beef Shanks

Prep time: 5 minutes | Cook time: 15 minutes |Serves 4

- 2 tablespoons olive oil
- 2 pounds beef shank
- Salt and black pepper to taste
- 1 onion, diced
- 2 stalks celery, diced
- 1 cup Marsala wine
- 2 tablespoons dried tarragon

1. Place the beef shanks in a baking pan.
2. Whisk the rest of the ingredients in a bowl and pour over the shanks.
3. Place these shanks in the air fry basket.
4. Transfer the basket to Ninja Foodi Dual Heat Air Fry Oven and close the door.
5. Select "Air Fry" mode by rotating the dial.
6. Press the TIME/SLICES button and change the value to 15 minutes.
7. Press the TEMP/SHADE button and change the value to 375 degrees F.
8. Press Start/Stop to begin cooking.
9. Serve warm.

Czech Roast Pork

Prep time: 5 minutes | Cook time: 3 hours 30 minutes |Serves 4

- 1 tablespoon caraway seeds
- ½ tablespoon garlic powder
- 1 tablespoon vegetable oil
- ½ tablespoon prepared mustard
- ½ tablespoon salt
- 1½ medium onions, chopped
- 2 pounds pork shoulder blade roast
- 1 teaspoon ground black pepper
- ¼ cup beer

1. Take a bowl and add garlic powder, mustard, vegetable oil, caraway seeds, salt and pepper to form a paste.
2. Rub the paste over pork roast and let it sit for about 30 minutes.
3. Turn on your Ninja Foodi Dual Heat Air Fry Oven and rotate the knob to select "Air Roast".
4. Preheat by selecting the timer for 3 minutes and temperature for 350 degrees F.
5. Take a SearPlate and add onions, pour in the beer and place pork.
6. Cover it with a foil.
7. Roast for about an hour in preheated Ninja Foodi Dual Heat Air Fry Oven at 350 degrees F.
8. Remove foil, turn roast and let it roast for 2 hours and 30 minutes more.
9. Remove from oven and set aside for 10 minutes before slicing.
10. Serve warm and enjoy!

Garlic Braised Ribs

Prep time: 5 minutes | Cook time: 20 minutes |Serves 8

- 2 tablespoons vegetable oil
- 5 pounds bone-in short ribs
- Salt and black pepper, to taste
- 2 heads garlic, halved
- 1 medium onion, chopped
- 4 ribs celery, chopped
- 2 medium carrots, chopped
- 3 tablespoons tomato paste
- ¼ cup dry red wine
- ¼ cup beef stock
- 4 sprigs thyme
- 1 cup parsley, chopped
- ½ cup chives, chopped
- 1 tablespoon lemon zest, grated

1. Toss everything in a large bowl, then add short ribs.
2. Mix well to soak the ribs and marinate for 30 minutes.
3. Transfer the soaked ribs to the SearPlate and add the marinade around them.
4. Transfer the SearPlate to Ninja Foodi Dual Heat Air Fry Oven and close the door.
5. Select "Air Fry" mode by rotating the dial.
6. Press the TIME/SLICES button and change the value to 20 minutes.
7. Press the TEMP/SHADE button and change the value to 400 degrees F.
8. Press Start/Stop to begin cooking.
9. Serve warm.

Lamb Chops With Carrots

Prep time: 5 minutes | Cook time: 10 minutes |Serves 4

- 2 tablespoons fresh rosemary, minced
- 2 tablespoons fresh mint leaves, minced
- 1 garlic clove, minced
- 3 tablespoons olive oil
- Salt and ground black pepper, as required
- 4 lamb chops
- 2 large carrots, peeled and cubed

1. In a large bowl, mix together the herbs, garlic, oil, salt, and black pepper.
2. Add the chops and generously coat with mixture.
3. Refrigerate to marinate for about 3 hours.
4. In a large pan of water, soak the carrots for about 15 minutes.
5. Drain the carrots completely.
6. Press AIR OVEN MODE button of Ninja Foodi Dual Heat Air Fry Oven and turn the dial to select "Air Fry" mode.
7. Press TIME/SLICES button and again turn the dial to set the cooking time to 10 minutes.
8. Now push TEMP/SHADE button and rotate the dial to set the temperature at 390 degrees F.
9. Press "Start/Stop" button to start.
10. When the unit beeps to show that it is preheated, open the oven door.
11. Arrange chops into the greased air fry basket in a single layer and insert in the oven.
12. After 2 minutes of cooking, arrange carrots into the air fry basket and top with the chops in a single layer.
13. Insert the basket in oven.
14. When the cooking time is completed, open the oven door and transfer the chops and carrots onto serving plates.
15. Serve hot.

Tex Mex Beef Stew

Prep time: 15 minutes | Cook time: 25 minutes | Serves 10

- 2 tsp cumin
- 1 tsp salt
- 1 tsp garlic powder
- 2 tbsp. coconut oil
- 1 lb. lean ground beef
- 1 lb. beef chuck, boneless & cut in 1-inch cubes
- 2 cups sweet onions, chopped
- 1 yellow bell pepper, seeded & chopped
- 1 orange bell pepper, seeded & chopped
- 1 sweet potato, peeled & chopped
- 2 28 oz. cans tomatoes, crushed
- 1 cup beef broth, low sodium
- 3 chipotle peppers in adobo sauce, chopped
- ¼ cup cilantro, chopped, divided

1. In a small bowl, combine cumin, salt, and garlic powder.
2. Add oil to the cooking pot and set to sauté on med-high heat.
3. Add the ground beef and half the spice mixture. Cook until beef is no longer pink. Use a slotted spoon to transfer beef to a bowl.
4. Add beef chuck and remaining spice mixture and cook until meat is browned on all sides.
5. Add the ground beef back to the pot. Add remaining ingredients, except cilantro, and stir to mix.
6. Add the lid and set to pressure cook on high. Set timer for 12 minutes. When the timer goes off, use manual release to remove the pressure. Stir in 2 tablespoons cilantro. Ladle into bowls and garnish with remaining cilantro. Serve.

Polish Sausage & Sauerkraut

Prep time: 10 minutes | Cook time: 7 hours | Serves 6

- 2 tbsp. olive oil
- 1 onion, chopped
- ½ lb. bacon, chopped
- ½ lb. smoked Polish sausage, cut in 1-inch pieces
- 1 head cabbage, chopped
- 1 lb. sauerkraut, rinsed & drained
- 1 cup beef broth, low sodium
- 2 bay leaves
- 1 cup dry red wine

1. Add the oil to the cooking pot and set to sauté on medium heat.
2. Add the onions and cook, stirring occasionally, until onions are golden. Use a slotted spoon to transfer onions to a bowl.
3. Add bacon to the pot and cook 2-3 minutes. Add sausage and cook until nicely browned, about 5 minutes. Use a slotted spoon to transfer meat to the bowl with onions. Drain off any remaining fat.
4. Add the cabbage, sauerkraut, and broth to the pot and mix well. Add the lid and set to slow cook on low. Cook 4 hours.
5. Stir in the onion mixture, bay leaves, and wine. Recover and cook another 2-3 hours until vegetables are tender. Discard bay leaves, stir and serve.

Maple Apples & Pork Chops

Prep time: 10 minutes | Cook time: 40 minutes | Serves 4

- nonstick cooking spray
- 2 Granny Smith apples, cored & sliced thin
- ¼ cup water
- ½ tsp cinnamon
- 1 tbsp. maple syrup, sugar free
- 4 pork chops, boneless

1. Spray the cooking pot with cooking spray. Set to sauté on medium heat.
2. Add the apples and cook until browned on both sides, stirring occasionally.
3. Add water and cinnamon, cover, and simmer 10-15 minutes or until apples are tender.
4. Remove lid, increase heat and cook, stirring until water has evaporated. Transfer apples to a bowl and stir in the syrup. Keep warm.
5. Spray the rack with cooking spray and place it in the pot. Place the pork chops on the plate and add the tender-crisp lid. Set to broil. Broil chops about 10 minutes per side.
6. Transfer chops to serving plates and top with apple mixture. Serve immediately.

Tangy Garlic Pork Loin

Prep time: 35 minutes | Cook time: 40 minutes | Serves 4

- 2 tbsp. fresh lime juice
- 1 tbsp. olive oil
- 3 green onions, sliced thin
- 1 tbsp. garlic, chopped fine
- 1 ½ tsp thyme
- ¼ tsp pepper
- 1 lb. pork tenderloin
- nonstick cooking spray

1. In a large bowl, combine lime juice, oil, green onion, garlic, thyme, and pepper, mix well.
2. Add the tenderloin and turn to coat. Cover and refrigerate 30 minutes.
3. Spray the cooking pot with cooking spray. Add the tenderloin to the pot, discard the marinade.
4. Add the tender-crisp lid and set to roast on 400°F. Cook tenderloin 35-40 minutes, or until it reaches desired doneness. Serve.

Chipotle Burgers

Prep time: 15 minutes | Cook time: 20 minutes | Serves 6

- nonstick cooking spray
- 2 poblano chilies
- 1 tsp. olive oil
- 1 ¼ tsp salt, divided
- 1 ½ lbs. lean ground beef
- 1/3 cup onion, grated
- 3 chipotle peppers in adobo sauce, chopped fine
- 1 tbsp. adobo sauce
- 1 tsp cumin
- 1 tsp pepper
- 6 slices jack cheese
- 6 hamburger buns
- 2 avocados, sliced
- 1/3 cup cilantro, chopped
- hot sauce, to taste

1. Spray the fryer basket with cooking spray and add to the cooking pot.
2. Place the whole poblano chilies in the basket. Add the tender-crisp lid and set to air fry on 400°F. Cook chilies until charred on all sides. Transfer chilies to Ziploc bag, seal, and let rest 15 minutes.
3. Remove the skins and seeds from the chilies. Slice them into ribbons and place in a medium bowl. Drizzle with oil and season with ¼ teaspoon salt, toss to coat. Cover until ready to use.
4. In a large bowl, combine ground beef, onion, chipotles, adobo sauce, remaining salt, cumin, and pepper. Mix until everything is combined. Form into 6 patties.
5. Spray the rack with cooking spray and place it in the cooking pot. Place the patties on the rack.
6. Add the tender-crisp lid and set to broil. Cook patties 6-7 minutes per side, or until patties reach desired doneness. Top each patty with cheese and broil until cheese is melted.
7. To serve, place patty on bottom bun, top with avocado and some of the roasted chilies, cilantro and hot sauce. Serve immediately.

Chinese BBQ Ribs

Prep time: 15 minutes | Cook time: 8 hours | Serves 6

- 4 tbsp. hoisin sauce
- 4 tbsp. oyster sauce
- 2 tbsp. soy sauce, low sodium
- 2 tbsp. rice wine
- 2 lbs. pork ribs, cut in 6 pieces
- nonstick cooking spray
- 2-inch piece fresh ginger, grated
- 3 green onions, sliced
- 2 tbsp. honey

1. In a large bowl, whisk together hoisin sauce, oyster sauce, soy sauce, and rice wine. Add the ribs and turn to coat. Cover and refrigerate overnight.
2. Spray the cooking pot with cooking spray.
3. Add the ribs and marinade. Top with ginger and green onions. Add the lid and set to slow cook on low. Cook 6-8 hours or until ribs are tender.
4. Transfer ribs to a serving plate. Spray the rack with the cooking spray and place in the pot. Lay the ribs, in a single layer, on the rack and brush with honey.
5. Add the tender-crisp lid and set to broil. Cook 3-4 minutes to caramelize the ribs. Serve.

Lone Star Chili

Prep time: 15 minutes | Cook time: 8 hours | Serves 8

- 2 tbsp. flour
- 2 lbs. lean beef chuck, cubed
- 1 tbsp. olive oil
- 1 onion, chopped fine
- 2 jalapeño peppers, chopped
- 4 cloves garlic, chopped fine
- 1 tbsp. cumin
- 4 oz. green chilies, drained & chopped
- 3 tbsp. Ancho chili powder

- 1 tsp crushed red pepper flakes
- 1 tsp oregano
- 3 cups beef broth, fat-free & low-sodium
- 28 oz. tomatoes, diced, undrained
- ¼ cup Greek yogurt, fat free
- 3 tbsp. green onions, chopped

1. Place the flour in a large Ziploc bag. Add the beef and toss to coat.
2. Add the beef and cook, stirring occasionally, until browned on all sides. Add the onions and jalapenos and cook until soft. Stir in the garlic and cook 1 minute more.
3. Stir in remaining ingredients, except yogurt and green onions, mix well. Add the lid and set to slow cook on low. Cook 7-8 hours until chili is thick and beef is tender.
4. Ladle into bowls and top with a dollop of yogurt and green onions. Serve.

Tender Butter Beef

Prep time: 5 minutes | Cook time: 8 hours | Serves 12

- 3 lbs. beef stew meat
- 1/3 cup butter
- 1 ¼ oz. dry onion soup mix
- ¼ cup beef broth, low sodium
- 1 tbsp. cornstarch

1. Place beef and butter the cooking pot. Sprinkle onion soup mix over the meat.
2. Add the lid and set to slow cook on low. Cook 7-8 hours, stirring occasionally, untl beef is tender.
3. In a small bowl, whisk together broth and cornstarch until smooth. Stir into beef mixture completely and let cook 10 minutes or until sauce has thickened. Serve over cooked rice or quinoa.

Bacon & Sauerkraut with Apples

Prep time: 10 minutes | Cook time: 30 minutes | Serves 6

- ¼ lb. apple-wood smoked bacon
- 1 onion, chopped fine
- 2 Granny Smith apples, peeled, cored, & grated
- 2 cloves garlic, chopped fine
- 1 tsp caraway seeds, ground
- 3 cups apple juice, unsweetened
- ¼ cup white wine vinegar
- 2 lbs. refrigerated sauerkraut, drained

1. Add the bacon to the cooking pot and set to sauté on medium heat. Cook until bacon has browned and fat is rendered. Transfer to paper towel lined plat. Drain all but 1 tablespoon of the fat.
2. Add the onions and apples to the pot and cook 6-7 minutes, until onions are translucent. Add the garlic and caraway and cook 1 minute more.
3. Stir in apple juice and vinegar, increase heat to med-high and bring to a boil. Let boil about 5 minutes until liquid is reduced to a syrup.
4. Chop the bacon and add it and the sauerkraut to the pot, stir to mix. Reduce heat to low and cook 10 minutes until heated through and sauerkraut is tender. Salt and pepper to taste and serve.

Southern Sweet Ham

Prep time: 5 minutes | Cook time: 8 hours | Serves 12

- 5 ½ lb. ham, bone-in & cooked
- 1 cup apple cider
- ½ cup dark brown sugar
- 1/3 cup bourbon
- ¼ cup honey
- ¼ cup Dijon mustard
- 4 sprigs fresh thyme

1. Place the ham in the cooking pot.
2. In a small bowl, whisk together cider, brown sugar, bourbon, honey, and mustard until smooth. Pour over the ham. Scatter the thyme around the ham.
3. Add the lid and set to slow cook on low. Cook 8 hours or until ham is very tender. Transfer ham to cutting board and let rest 10-15 minutes.
4. Pour the cooking liquid through fine mesh sieve into a bowl. Pour back into the cooking pot. Set to sauté on med-high heat and bring to a simmer, cook 10 minutes or until reduced, stirring occasionally.
5. Slice the ham and serve topped with sauce.

Chapter 5

Poultry Recipes

Crispy Chicken Cutlets

Prep time: 5 minutes | Cook time: 30 minutes
|Serves 4

- ¾ cup flour
- 2 large eggs
- 1½ cups breadcrumbs
- ¼ cup Parmesan cheese, grated
- 1 tablespoon mustard powder
- Salt and ground black pepper, as required
- 4 (¼-inch thick) skinless, boneless chicken cutlets

1. In a shallow bowl, add the flour.
2. In a second bowl, crack the eggs and beat well.
3. In a third bowl, mix together the breadcrumbs, cheese, mustard powder, salt, and black pepper.
4. Season the chicken with salt, and black pepper.
5. Coat the chicken with flour, then dip into beaten eggs and finally coat with the breadcrumbs mixture.
6. Press AIR OVEN MODE button of Ninja Foodi Dual Heat Air Fry Oven and turn the dial to select "Air Fry" mode.
7. Press TIME/SLICES button and again turn the dial to set the cooking time to 30 minutes.
8. Now push TEMP/SHADE button and rotate the dial to set the temperature at 355 degrees F.
9. Press "Start/Stop" button to start.
10. When the unit beeps to show that it is preheated, open the oven door and grease the air fry basket.
11. Place the chicken cutlets into the prepared air fry basket and insert in the oven.
12. When cooking time is completed, open the oven door and serve hot.

Crispy Chicken Legs

Prep time: 5 minutes | Cook time: 20 minutes
|Serves 3

- 3 chicken legs
- 1 cup buttermilk
- 2 cups white flour
- 1 teaspoon garlic powder
- 1 teaspoon onion powder
- 1 teaspoon ground cumin
- 1 teaspoon paprika
- Salt and ground black pepper, as required
- 1 tablespoon olive oil

1. In a bowl, place the chicken legs and buttermilk and refrigerate for about 2 hours.
2. In a shallow dish, mix together the flour and spices.
3. Remove the chicken from buttermilk.
4. Coat the chicken legs with flour mixture, then dip into buttermilk and finally, coat with the flour mixture again.
5. Press AIR OVEN MODE button of Ninja Foodi Dual Heat Air Fry Oven and turn the dial to select "Air Fry" mode.
6. Press TIME/SLICES button and again turn the dial to set the cooking time to 20 minutes.
7. Now push TEMP/SHADE button and rotate the dial to set the temperature at 355 degrees F.
8. Press "Start/Stop" button to start.
9. When the unit beeps to show that it is preheated, open the oven door and grease the air fry basket.
10. Arrange chicken legs into the prepared air fry basket and drizzle with the oil.
11. Insert the basket in the oven.
12. When cooking time is completed, open the oven door and serve hot.

Thanksgiving Turkey

Prep time: 5 minutes | Cook time: 35 minutes |Serves 4

- 1 turkey breast
- Kosher salt and black pepper, to taste
- 1 teaspoon thyme, chopped
- 1 teaspoon rosemary, chopped
- 1 teaspoon sage, chopped
- ¼ cup maple syrup
- 2 tablespoons Dijon mustard
- 1 tablespoon. butter, melted

1. Rub the turkey breast with maple syrup, Dijon mustard, butter, black pepper, and herbs.
2. Place the turkey in a baking tray and set it in the Ninja Foodi Digital Air Fry Oven.
3. Select the "AIR CRISP" mode using the function keys.
4. Set its cooking time to 35 minutes and temperature to 390 degrees F
5. Press "START/PAUSE" to initiate preheating.
6. Serve warm.

Tasty Chicken Drumsticks

Prep time: 5 minutes | Cook time: 20 minutes |Serves 4

- 4 chicken drumsticks
- 3/4 cup teriyaki sauce
- 4 tbsp green onion, chopped
- 1 tbsp sesame seeds, toasted

1. Select air fry mode set the temperature to 360 F and set the timer to 20 minutes. Press the setting dial to preheat.
2. Add chicken drumsticks and teriyaki sauce into the zip-lock bag. Seal bag and place in refrigerator for 1 hour.
3. Arrange marinated chicken drumsticks in the air fryer basket.

4. Once the unit is preheated, open the door, and place the air fryer basket on the top level of the oven, and close the door.
5. Garnish with green onion and sprinkle with sesame seeds.
6. Serve and enjoy.

Chicken Stew

Prep time: 5 minutes | Cook time: 1 hour and 10 minutes |Serves 6

- 1 rotisserie chicken, roughly shredded
- 1 package precooked chicken sausages, sliced
- 3 medium carrots, diced
- 1 bag frozen pearl onions
- 1 can cannellini beans, drained and rinsed
- 3 garlic cloves, minced
- 2 cups chicken stock
- Kosher salt and freshly ground black pepper, to taste

1. In a large bowl, combine the chicken, sausages, carrots, pearl onions, beans, garlic, stock, salt, and pepper. Pour the mixture into a casserole dish.
2. Select "AIR ROAST," on your Ninja Foodi Digital Air Fry Oven.
3. Set the temperature to 325 degrees F, and set the time to 60 minutes.
4. Press "START/PAUSE" to begin preheating.
5. When the unit has preheated, place the casserole dish on the wire rack inside.
6. Close the oven door to begin cooking.
7. When cooking is completed, let the stew cool for 10 minutes before serving.

Tasty Chicken Wings

Prep time: 5 minutes | Cook time: 12 minutes |Serves 6

- 6 chicken wings
- 1/2 tsp red chili flakes
- 1 tbsp honey
- 2 tbsp Worcestershire sauce
- Pepper
- Salt

1. Add all ingredients except chicken wings to a bowl and mix well.
2. Arrange chicken wings in an air fryer basket.
3. Select air fry then set the temperature to 350 F and time for 12 minutes. Press start.
4. Once the oven is preheated then place the basket into the top rails of the oven.
5. Serve and enjoy.

Lemon Pepper Baked Chicken

Prep time: 5 minutes | Cook time: 30 minutes |Serves 4

- 4 chicken breasts, skinless and boneless
- 1 tsp lemon pepper seasoning
- 4 tsp lemon juice
- 4 tsp butter, sliced
- 1/2 tsp paprika
- 1 tsp garlic powder
- Pepper
- Salt

1. Place rack in the bottom position and close door. Select bake mode set the temperature to 350 F and set the timer to 30 minutes. Press the setting dial to preheat.
2. Season chicken with pepper and salt and place in the baking dish.
3. Pour lemon juice over chicken.

4. Mix together paprika, lemon pepper seasoning, and garlic powder and sprinkle over chicken.
5. Add butter slices on top of the chicken.
6. Once the unit is preheated, open the door, and place the baking dish onto the center of the rack, and close the door.
7. Serve and enjoy.

Deviled Chicken

Prep time: 5 minutes | Cook time: 40 minutes |Serves 8

- 2 tablespoons butter
- 2 cloves garlic, chopped
- 1 cup Dijon mustard
- ½ teaspoon cayenne pepper
- 1 ½ cups panko breadcrumbs
- ¾ cup Parmesan, freshly grated
- ¼ cup chives, chopped
- 2 teaspoons paprika
- 8 small bone-in chicken thighs, skin removed

1. Toss the chicken thighs with crumbs, cheese, chives, butter, and spices in a bowl and mix well to coat.
2. Transfer the chicken along with its spice mix to a SearPlate.
3. Transfer the SearPlate to Ninja Foodi Dual Heat Air Fry Oven and close the door.
4. Select "Air Fry" mode by rotating the dial.
5. Press the TIME/SLICES button and change the value to 40 minutes.
6. Press the TEMP/SHADE button and change the value to 375 degrees F.
7. Press Start/Stop to begin cooking.
8. Serve warm.

Sour Cream & Cheese Chicken

Prep time: 5 minutes | Cook time: 25 minutes | Serves 8

- nonstick cooking spray
- 1 cup sour cream
- 2 tsp garlic powder
- 1 tsp seasoned salt
- ½ tsp pepper
- 1 ½ cups parmesan cheese, divided
- 3 lbs. chicken breasts, boneless

1. Spray the cooking pot with cooking spray.
2. In a medium bowl, combine sour cream, garlic powder, seasoned salt, pepper, and 1 cup parmesan cheese, mix well.
3. Place the chicken in the cooking pot. Spread the sour cream mixture over the top and sprinkle with remaining parmesan cheese.
4. Add the tender-crisp lid and set to bake on 375°F. Bake chicken 25-30 minutes until cooked through.
5. Set cooker to broil and cook another 2-3 minutes until top is lightly browned. Serve immediately.

Air Fried Whole Chicken

Prep time: 5 minutes | Cook time:60 minutes |Serves 10

- 1 whole chicken, giblets removed
- 2 tablespoons avocado oil
- 1 tablespoon kosher salt
- 1 teaspoon black pepper
- 1 teaspoon garlic powder
- 1 teaspoon paprika
- ½ teaspoon dried basil
- ½ teaspoon dried oregano
- ½ teaspoon dried thyme

1. Rub the chicken with avocado oil, salt, black pepper, garlic powder, paprika, basil, oregano, and thyme. Place the seasoned chicken in a baking tray.
2. Set the baking tray in the Ninja Foodi Digital Air Fry Oven and close its door.
3. Set its cooking time to 50 minutes and temperature to 360 degrees F, then press "START/PAUSE" to initiate preheating.
4. Flip the whole chicken and cook for another 10 minutes.
5. Serve warm.

Cheesy Chicken & Mushrooms

Prep time: 5 minutes | Cook time: 30 minutes | Serves 4

- nonstick cooking spray
- 1 ½ cups mushrooms, sliced
- ¼ cup ham, chopped
- 4 chicken breasts, boneless & skinless
- ¼ tsp pepper
- 1 can cream of chicken soup, reduced fat
- ½ tsp thyme
- ½ tsp onion powder
- ¼ cup mozzarella cheese, grated

1. Spray the cooking pot with cooking spray.
2. Set to sauté on med-high heat. Add the mushrooms and ham and cook, stirring occasionally, until mushrooms start to brown, about 5-7 minutes. Transfer to a bowl.
3. Season both sides of the chicken with garlic powder and pepper. Place in the pot. Spoon the mushroom mixture over the top.
4. In a medium bowl, whisk together soup, milk, thyme, and onion powder. Pour over mushrooms and top with cheese.
5. Add the tender-crisp lid and set to bake on 350°F. Cook 25-30 minutes until chicken is cooked through. Serve.

Cheesy Chipotle Chicken

Prep time: 10 minutes | Cook time: 35 minutes | Serves 6

- 15 oz. fire roasted tomatoes
- ¼ cup red onion, chopped
- 1 clove garlic
- ½ cup cilantro, chopped, packed
- 2 chipotle chili peppers in adobo sauce
- 1 tsp adobo sauce
- 1 tsp fresh lime juice
- 1 tsp salt
- 1½ lbs. chicken, cut in 3-inch pieces
- 1 cup Monterey Jack cheese, grated

1. Add the tomatoes, onion, garlic, cilantro, chipotle peppers, lime juice, and salt to a food processor or blender. Pulse until vegetables are chopped but not until the salsa is smooth.
2. Place the chicken in the cooking pot. Pour the salsa over the tops. Turn the chicken to coat with salsa on all sides.
3. Add the tender-crisp lid and set to bake on 350°F. Bake 25 minutes. Remove the lid and sprinkle the cheese over the top.
4. Recover and bake another 10 minutes or until chicken is cooked through and cheese is melted and starting to brown. Serve.

Chicken Cutlets in Dijon Sauce

Prep time: 10 minutes | Cook time: 15 minutes | Serves 2

- 2 chicken breasts, boneless & skinless
- 2 tbsp. olive oil, divided
- ½ tsp salt
- ¼ tsp pepper
- ½ tbsp. lemon zest
- 1 clove garlic, chopped fine
- 1 tbsp. fresh rosemary, chopped

- 1 tbsp. fresh parsley, chopped
- 2 tbsp. flour
- nonstick cooking spray
- 1 shallot, sliced thin
- ½ lemon, juiced
- ½ cup dry white wine
- 1 tsp Dijon mustard

1. Place chicken between 2 pieces of plastic wrap and pound to ½-inch thick. Place them in a large bowl.
2. Top the chicken with oil, salt, pepper, zest, garlic, rosemary, and parsley. Cover and refrigerate 1 hour or overnight.
3. Place the flour in a shallow dish and dredge both sides of chicken. Let sit 2-3 minutes.
4. Lightly spray the fryer basket with cooking spray. Place the chicken in the basket and add the tender-crisp lid. Set to air fry on 350 °F. Cook chicken 3-5 minutes per side until golden brown and cooked through. Transfer to plate and keep warm.
5. Set cooker to sauté on medium heat. Add the oil and shallot and cook until shallot softens. Stir in lemon juice, wine, and mustard and cook until reduced slightly, about 2-3 minutes.
6. Transfer chicken to serving plates and top with sauce. Serve immediately.

Spiced Turkey Breast

Prep time: 5 minutes | Cook time: 45 minutes |Serves 8

- 2 tablespoons fresh rosemary, chopped
- 1 teaspoon ground cumin
- 1 teaspoon ground cinnamon
- 1 teaspoon smoked paprika
- 1 teaspoon cayenne pepper
- Salt and ground black pepper, as required
- 1 turkey breast

1. In a bowl, mix together the rosemary, spices, salt and black pepper.
2. Rub the turkey breast with rosemary mixture evenly.
3. With kitchen twines, tie the turkey breast to keep it compact.
4. Press AIR OVEN MODE button of Ninja Foodi Dual Heat Air Fry Oven and turn the dial to select "Air Fry" mode.
5. Press TIME/SLICES button and again turn the dial to set the cooking time to 45 minutes.
6. Now push TEMP/SHADE button and rotate the dial to set the temperature at 360 degrees F.
7. Press "Start/Stop" button to start.
8. When the unit beeps to show that it is preheated, open the oven door.
9. Arrange the turkey breast into the greased air fry basket and insert in oven.
10. When the cooking time is completed, open the oven door and place the turkey breast onto a platter for about 5-10 minutes before slicing.
11. With a sharp knife, cut the turkey breast into desired sized slices and serve.

Turkey Stroganoff

Prep time: 10 minutes | Cook time: 30 minutes | Serves 4

- nonstick cooking spray
- 12 oz. turkey breast, cut in thin strips
- ½ cup onion, chopped
- 2 large Portobello mushrooms, remove stems & slice thin
- 1 tbsp. olive oil
- 2 tbsp. flour
- 1 ¾ cup chicken broth, low sodium
- ½ cup sour cream, fat free
- 1 ½ tsp Dijon mustard
- 1 tsp fresh parsley, chopped
- 8 ounces medium egg noodles, cooked & drained

1. Spray the cooking pot with cooking spray and set to sauté on medium heat.
2. Add turkey and onion and cook 5 minutes, stirring frequently, until onion is soft.
3. Add mushrooms and cook 3-4 minutes until turkey is no longer pink and mushrooms are tender. Transfer to a bowl.
4. Add the oil and flour and cook, stirring, 1 minute. Stir in the broth and cook 4-5 minutes or until thickened.
5. Reduce heat to low and add sour cream, mustard, and parsley, mix well. Return the turkey mixture to the pot and cook 2-3 minutes or until heated through.
6. Divide noodles between serving plates and top with stroganoff. Serve.

Honey Chicken & Veggies

Prep time: 15 minutes | Cook time: 6 hours | Serves 6

- ½ cup honey
- 1/3 cup balsamic vinegar
- 3 tbsp. tomato paste
- ½ tsp salt
- ½ tsp pepper
- 3 cloves garlic, chopped fine
- 1 tsp ginger
- ¼ tsp red pepper flakes
- 6 chicken thighs
- 2 cups baby carrots
- 2 cups baby red potatoes, quartered
- 1 tbsp. fresh parsley, chopped

1. In a small bowl, whisk together honey, vinegar, tomato paste, salt, pepper, garlic, ginger, and pepper flakes until combined.
2. Add chicken, carrots, and potatoes to the cooking pot.
3. Pour honey mixture over the top, reserving ½ cup. Toss gently to mix.
4. Add the lid and set to slow cook on low. Cook 6-8 hours until vegetables are tender and chicken is cooked through.
5. Pour remaining glaze over chicken and vegetables and serve garnished with parsley.

Pineapple Chicken Tenders

Prep time: 20 minutes | Cook time: 15 minutes | Serves 4

- 1 lb. chicken tenders
- ½ cup stir-fry sauce
- 1 tbsp. olive oil
- ½ red bell pepper, chopped
- ½ yellow bell pepper, chopped
- ½ green bell pepper, chopped
- ¼ cup green onions, sliced
- 8 oz. pineapple chunks or tidbits, juice reserved

1. Combine chicken and stir fry sauce in a large Ziploc bag. Seal and turn to coat the chicken. Refrigerate 20 minutes.
2. 2 Add the oil to the cooking pot and set to sauté on med-high heat.
3. Add the chicken and cook 6-8 minutes or until cooked through. Transfer chicken to a plate and keep warm.
4. Add the peppers to the pot and cook 4-5 minutes until tender-crisp.
5. Add the green onions, pineapple, 1 tablespoon pineapple juice and 2 teaspoons marinade and cook, stirring about 1 minute. Spoon over chicken and serve immediately.

Riviera Chicken

Prep time: 5 minutes | Cook time: 20 minutes | Serves 4

- nonstick cooking spray
- 4 chicken breast halves, boneless & skinless
- 1/8 tsp salt
- 1/8 tsp pepper
- 14 ½ oz. tomatoes with basil, garlic, and oregano, diced
- ½ cup black olives, sliced
- 1 tbsp. lemon zest, grated fine
- 2 cloves garlic, chopped fine

1. Spray the cooking pot with cooking spray and set to sauté on med-high heat.
2. Season chicken with salt and pepper and add to the pot. Cook 5-7 minutes per side, until no longer pink. Transfer chicken to a plate and reduce heat to medium.
3. Add remaining ingredients to the pot and cook 4 minutes or until hot, stirring occasionally. Return the chicken to the pot and cook until heated through. Serve immediately.

Chapter 6

Fish & Seafood Recipes

Lemony Salmon

Prep time: 5 minutes | Cook time: 8 minutes |Serves 3

- 1½ pounds salmon
- ½ teaspoon red chili powder
- Salt and ground black pepper, as required
- 1 lemon, cut into slices
- 1 tablespoon fresh dill, chopped

1. Season the salmon with chili powder, salt, and black pepper.
2. Press AIR OVEN MODE button of Ninja Foodi Dual Heat Air Fry Oven and turn the dial to select "Air Fry" mode.
3. Press TIME/SLICES button and again turn the dial to set the cooking time to 8 minutes.
4. Now push TEMP/SHADE button and rotate the dial to set the temperature at 375 degrees F.
5. Press "Start/Stop" button to start.
6. When the unit beeps to show that it is preheated, open the oven door.
7. Arrange the salmon fillets into the greased air fry basket and insert in the oven.
8. When cooking time is completed, open the oven door and serve hot with the garnishing of fresh dill.

Fish Newburg With Haddock

Prep time: 5 minutes | Cook time: 29 minutes |Serves 4

- 1 ½ pounds haddock fillets
- Salt and freshly ground black pepper
- 4 tablespoons butter
- 1 tablespoon & 2 teaspoons flour
- ¼ teaspoon sweet paprika
- ¼ teaspoon ground nutmeg
- Dash cayenne pepper
- ¾ cup heavy cream
- ½ cup milk
- 3 tablespoons dry sherry
- 2 large egg yolks
- 4 pastry shells

1. Rub haddock with black pepper and salt, then place in a SearPlate.
2. Place the spiced haddock in the pastry shell and close it like a calzone.
3. Drizzle 1 tablespoon of melted butter on top. Transfer the SearPlate to Ninja Foodi Dual Heat Air Fry Oven and close the door.
4. Select "Bake" mode by rotating the dial.
5. Press the TIME/SLICES button and change the value to 25 minutes.
6. Press the TEMP/SHADE button and change the value to 350 degrees F.
7. Press Start/Stop to begin cooking.
8. Meanwhile, melt 3 tablespoons of butter in a suitable saucepan over low heat.
9. Stir in nutmeg, cayenne, paprika, and salt, then mix well.
10. Add flour to the spice butter and whisk well to avoid lumps.
11. Cook for 2 minutes, then add milk and cream. Mix well and cook until thickens.
12. Beat egg yolks with sherry in a bowl and stir in a ladle of cream mixture.
13. Mix well and return the mixture to the saucepan.
14. Cook the mixture on low heat for 2 minutes.
15. Add the baked wrapped haddock to the sauce and cook until warm.
16. Serve warm.

Herb Salmon

**Prep time: 5 minutes | Cook time: 15 minutes
|Serves 4**

- 1 lbs salmon, cut into 4 pieces
- 1/4 tsp dried basil
- 1 tbsp olive oil
- 1/2 tbsp dried rosemary
- Pepper
- Salt

1. Place salmon pieces in an air fryer basket.
2. In a small bowl, mix together olive oil, basil, and rosemary.
3. Brush salmon with oil mixture.
4. Place the basket in the oven.
5. Select air fry then set the temperature to 400 F and time for 15 minutes. Press start.
6. Once the oven is preheated then place the basket into the top rails of the oven.
7. Serve and enjoy.

Pesto Fish Fillets

**Prep time: 5 minutes | Cook time: 10 minutes
|Serves 4**

- 4 tilapia fillets
- 2 tbsp olive oil
- For pesto:
- 2/3 cup basil
- 1/2 cup olive oil
- 2 tbsp parmesan cheese, shredded
- 4 tbsp pine nuts
- 2 garlic cloves
- Pepper
- Salt

1. Select air fry mode set the temperature to 350 F and set the timer to 10 minutes. Press the setting dial to preheat.
2. Brush fish fillets with oil and season with pepper and salt.
3. Arrange fish fillets in the air fryer basket.

4. Once the unit is preheated, open the door, and place the air fryer basket on the top level of the oven, and close the door.
5. Add all pesto ingredients into the blender and blend until smooth.
6. Pour pesto over fish fillets and serve.

Spicy Shrimp

**Prep time: 5 minutes | Cook time: 8 minutes
|Serves 4**

- 1 lb shrimp, peeled and deveined
- 1 tbsp soy sauce
- 3 tbsp butter, melted
- 1 tsp garlic, chopped
- 1 tbsp chili paste

1. Add shrimp into the baking dish.
2. In a bowl, mix together butter, soy sauce, chili paste, and garlic and pour over shrimp and mix well.
3. Select bake mode then set the temperature to 400 F and time for 8 minutes. Press start.
4. Once the oven is preheated then place the baking dish into the oven.
5. Serve and enjoy.

Tangy Sea Bass

Prep time: 5 minutes | Cook time: 12 minutes |Serves 2

- 2 sea bass fillets
- 1 garlic clove, minced
- 1 teaspoon fresh dill, minced
- 1 tablespoon olive oil
- 1 tablespoon balsamic vinegar
- Salt and black pepper, to taste

1. In a large resealable bag, add all the ingredients. Seal the bag and shake well to mix.
2. Refrigerate to marinate for at least 30 minutes.
3. Remove the fish fillets from bag and shake off the excess marinade.
4. Arrange the fish fillets onto the greased sheet pan in a single layer.
5. Select "BAKE" function on your Ninja Foodi Digital Air Fry Oven.
6. Set the temperature at 450 degrees F. and the cooking time to 12 minutes.
7. Press the "START/PAUSE" button to start.
8. Insert the sheet pan into the oven.
9. When cooking time is completed, open the Flip the fish fillets once halfway through.
10. When cooking time is completed, open the door and serve hot.

Prawns In Butter Sauce

Prep time: 5 minutes | Cook time: 6 minutes |Serves 2

- ½ pound large prawns, peeled and deveined
- 1 large garlic clove, minced
- 1 tablespoon butter, melted
- 1 teaspoon fresh lemon zest, grated

1. In a bowl, add all the ingredients and toss to coat well.
2. Set aside at room temperature for about 30 minutes.
3. Arrange the prawn mixture into a SearPlate.
4. Press AIR OVEN MODE button of Ninja Foodi Dual Heat Air Fry Oven and turn the dial to select "Bake" mode.
5. Press TIME/SLICES button and again turn the dial to set the cooking time to 6 minutes.
6. Now push TEMP/SHADE button and rotate the dial to set the temperature at 450 degrees F.
7. Press "Start/Stop" button to start.
8. When the unit beeps to show that it is preheated, open the oven door.
9. Insert the SearPlate in the oven. Close the oven and let it cook.
10. When cooking time is completed, open the oven door and serve immediately.

Fish In Yogurt Marinade

Prep time: 5 minutes | Cook time: 10 minutes
|Serves 2

- 1 cup plain Greek yogurt
- Finely grated zest of 1 lemon
- 1 tablespoon lemon juice
- 1 tablespoon finely minced garlic
- 3 tablespoons fresh oregano leaves
- 1 teaspoon ground cumin
- ¼ teaspoon ground allspice
- ½ teaspoon salt
- ½ teaspoon freshly ground black pepper
- 1½ pounds perch filets

1. Mix lemon zest, yogurt, garlic, cumin, oregano, black pepper, salt, and all spices in SearPlate.
2. Add fish to this marinade, mix well to coat then cover it with a plastic wrap.
3. Marinate for 15 minutes in the refrigerator, then uncover.
4. Transfer the SearPlate to Ninja Foodi Dual Heat Air Fry Oven and close the door.
5. Select "Bake" mode by rotating the dial.
6. Press the TIME/SLICES button and change the value to 10 minutes.
7. Press the TEMP/SHADE button and change the value to 450 degrees F.
8. Press Start/Stop to begin cooking.
9. Serve warm.

Italian Salmon

Prep time: 5 minutes | Cook time: 20 minutes
|Serves 5

- 1 3/4 lbs salmon fillet
- 1 tbsp fresh dill, chopped
- 1/4 cup capers
- 1/3 cup artichoke hearts
- 1/3 cup basil pesto
- 1/4 cup sun-dried tomatoes, drained
- 1/4 cup olives, pitted and chopped

- 1 tsp paprika
- 1/4 tsp salt

1. Spray sheet pan with cooking spray.
2. Arrange salmon fillet on a greased sheet pan. Season with paprika and salt.
3. Add remaining ingredients on top of salmon.
4. Select bake mode then set the temperature to 400 F and time for 20 minutes. Press start.
5. Once the oven is preheated then place the sheet pan into the oven.
6. Serve and enjoy.

Sweet & Spicy Salmon

Prep time: 5 minutes | Cook time: 8 minutes
|Serves 4

- 4 salmon fillets
- 1 tsp smoked paprika
- 1 tsp chili powder
- 4 tbsp honey
- 1/2 tsp red pepper flakes, crushed
- 1/2 tsp garlic powder
- Pepper
- Salt

1. Select air fry mode set the temperature to 390 F and set the timer to 8 minutes. Press the setting dial to preheat.
2. In a small bowl, mix honey, chili powder, paprika, garlic powder, red pepper flakes, pepper, and salt.
3. Brush fish fillets with honey mixture and place into the air fryer basket.
4. Once the unit is preheated, open the door, and place the air fryer basket on the top level of the oven, and close the door.
5. Serve and enjoy.

Lobster Tails With Lemon-garlic Butter

Prep time: 5 minutes | Cook time: 10 minutes |Serves 1

- 2 tablespoons butter
- ½ teaspoon lemon zest
- 1 lobster tail
- ½ clove garlic, grated
- ½ teaspoon parsley, chopped
- Salt, to taste
- Fresh ground black pepper, to taste

1. Cut the lobster tail lengthwise through the center of the hard top shell.
2. Cut to the bottom of the shell and spread the tail halves apart.
3. Place the lobster tail in the air fry basket.
4. Take a saucepan and melt butter on medium heat.
5. Add garlic and lemon zest and cook for 30 seconds.
6. Now, pour the butter mixture onto lobster tail.
7. Turn on your Ninja Foodi Dual Heat Air Fry Oven and rotate the knob to select "Air Fry".
8. Select the timer for about 5 to 7 minutes and temperature for 380 degrees F.
9. Let it cook and serve with parsley as topping.

Arroz Con Cod

Prep time: 10 minutes | Cook time: 30 minutes | Serves 4

- ¼ cup olive oil
- 2 tbsp. garlic, chopped
- ½ cup red onion, chopped
- ½ cup red bell pepper, chopped
- ½ cup green bell pepper, chopped
- 2 cups long grain rice
- 3 tbsp. tomato paste
- 2 tsp turmeric
- 2 tbsp. cumin
- ½ tsp salt
- ¼ tsp pepper
- 4 cups chicken broth
- 1 bay leaf
- 1 lb. cod, cut in bite-size pieces
- ½ cup peas, cooked
- 4 tbsp. pimento, chopped
- 4 tsp cilantro, chopped

1. Add the oil to the cooking pot and set to sauté on med-high.
2. Add the garlic, onion, and peppers, and cook, stirring frequently for 2 minutes.
3. Stir in rice, tomato paste, and seasonings, and cook another 2 minutes.
4. Add the broth and bay leaf and bring to a boil. Reduce heat, cover, and let simmer 5 minutes.
5. Add the fish, recover the pot and cook 15-20 minutes until all the liquid is absorbed. Turn off the cooker and let sit for 5 minutes.
6. To serve: spoon onto plates and top with cooked peas, pimento and cilantro.

Garlic Shrimp

Prep time: 10 minutes | Cook time: 5 minutes | Serves 8

- nonstick cooking spray
- 1 lb. large shrimp, peeled & deveined
- 2 tbsp. butter, melted
- 4 cloves garlic, chopped fine
- ¼ cup fresh parsley, chopped
- ¼ tsp salt
- 1 tbsp. fresh lemon juice

1. Spray the fryer basket with cooking oil.
2. Add the shrimp to the basket.
3. Add the tender-crisp lid and set to air fry on 350°F. Cook 3-5 minutes until all the shrimp turn pink, stirring them after 2 minutes. Serve immediately.

Basil Lemon Shrimp & Asparagus

Prep time: 10 minutes | Cook time: 10 minutes | Serves 4

- 3 tbsp. water, divided
- 2 cloves garlic, chopped fine
- 2 tbsp. onion, chopped fine
- ½ tsp fresh ginger, grated
- ½ tsp salt
- ¼ tsp pepper
- ¼ tsp red pepper flakes
- 1 tbsp. fresh lemon juice
- 1 tsp lemon zest
- 3 tbsp. fresh basil, chopped

1. Add 2 tablespoons water, garlic, and onion to the cooking pot and set to sauté on medium heat. Cook 1 minute, stirring.
2. Add remaining water, ginger, salt, pepper, red pepper flakes, lemon juice, and asparagus, stir to combine. Add the lid and cook 2-3 minutes until asparagus starts to turn bright green.
3. Add the shrimp and stir. Recover and cook another 3-5 minutes or until shrimp are pink and asparagus is fork-tender.
4. Stir in the lemon zest and basil and serve.

Shrimp Fried Rice

Prep time: 5 minutes | Cook time: 15 minutes | Serves 6

- 2 tbsp. sesame oil
- 2 tbsp. olive oil
- 1 lb. medium shrimp, peeled & deveined
- 1 cup frozen peas & carrots
- 1/2 cup corn
- 3 cloves garlic, chopped fine
- ½ tsp ginger
- 3 eggs, lightly beaten
- 4 cups brown rice, cooked
- 3 green onions, sliced
- 3 tbsp. tamari
- ½ tsp salt
- ½ tsp pepper

1. Add the sesame and olive oils to the cooking pot and set to sauté on med-high heat.
2. Add the shrimp and cook 3 minutes, or until they turn pink, turning shrimp over halfway through. Use a slotted spoon to transfer shrimp to a plate.
3. Add the peas, carrots, and corn to the pot and cook 2 minutes until vegetables start to soften, stirring occasionally. Add the garlic and ginger and cook 1 minute more.
4. Push the vegetables to one side and add the eggs, cook to scramble, stirring frequently. Add the shrimp, rice, and onions and stir to mix all ingredients together.
5. Drizzle with tamari and season with salt and pepper, stir to combine. Cook 2 minutes or until everything is heated through. Serve immediately.

Chapter 7

Vegetables & Sides Recipes

Roasted Vegetables

**Prep time: 5 minutes | Cook time: 15 minutes
|Serves 6**

- 2 medium bell peppers cored, chopped
- 2 medium carrots, peeled and sliced
- 1 small zucchini, ends trimmed, sliced
- 1 medium broccoli, florets
- ½ red onion, peeled and diced
- 2 tablespoons olive oil
- 1 ½ teaspoons Italian seasoning
- 2 garlic cloves, minced
- Salt and freshly ground black pepper
- 1 cup grape tomatoes
- 1 tablespoon fresh lemon juice

1. Toss all the veggies with olive oil, Italian seasoning, salt, black pepper, and garlic in a large salad bowl.
2. Spread this broccoli-zucchini mixture in the SearPlate.
3. Transfer the SearPlate to Ninja Foodi Dual Heat Air Fry Oven and close the door.
4. Select "Bake" mode by rotating the dial.
5. Press the TIME/SLICES button and change the value to 15 minutes.
6. Press the TEMP/SHADE button and change the value to 400 degrees F.
7. Press Start/Stop to begin cooking.
8. Serve warm with lemon juice on top.
9. Enjoy.

Veggies Stuffed Bell Peppers

**Prep time: 5 minutes | Cook time: 25 minutes
|Serves 6**

- 6 large bell peppers
- 1 bread roll, finely chopped
- 1 carrot, peeled and finely chopped
- 1 onion, finely chopped
- 1 potato, peeled and finely chopped
- ½ cup fresh peas, shelled
- 2 garlic cloves, minced
- 2 teaspoons fresh parsley, chopped
- Salt and ground black pepper, as required
- ⅓ cup cheddar cheese, grated

1. Remove the tops of each bell pepper and discard the seeds.
2. Chop the bell pepper tops finely.
3. In a bowl, place bell pepper tops, bread loaf, vegetables, garlic, parsley, salt and black pepper and mix well.
4. Stuff each bell pepper with the vegetable mixture.
5. Press AIR OVEN MODE button of Ninja Foodi Dual Heat Air Fry Oven and turn the dial to select "Air Fry" mode.
6. Press TIME/SLICES button and again turn the dial to set the cooking time to 25 minutes.
7. Now push TEMP/SHADE button and rotate the dial to set the temperature at 330 degrees F.
8. Press "Start/Stop" button to start.
9. When the unit beeps to show that it is preheated, open the oven door.
10. Arrange the bell peppers into the greased air fry basket and insert in the oven.
11. After 20 minutes, sprinkle each bell pepper with cheddar cheese.
12. When cooking time is completed, open the oven door and transfer the bell peppers onto serving plates.
13. Serve hot.

Cauliflower In Buffalo Sauce

Prep time: 5 minutes | Cook time: 12 minutes
|Serves 4

- 1 large head cauliflower, cut into bite-size florets
- 1 tablespoon olive oil
- 2 teaspoons garlic powder
- Salt and ground black pepper, as required
- ⅔ cup warm buffalo sauce

1. In a large bowl, add cauliflower florets, olive oil, garlic powder, salt and pepper and toss to coat.
2. Press AIR OVEN MODE button of Ninja Foodi Dual Heat Air Fry Oven and turn the dial to select "Air Fry" mode.
3. Press TIME/SLICES button and again turn the dial to set the cooking time to 12 minutes.
4. Now push TEMP/SHADE button and rotate the dial to set the temperature at 375 degrees F.
5. Press "Start/Stop" button to start.
6. When the unit beeps to show that it is preheated, open the oven door.
7. Arrange the cauliflower florets in the air fry basket and insert in the oven.
8. After 7 minutes of cooking, coat the cauliflower florets with buffalo sauce.
9. When cooking time is completed, open the oven door and serve hot.

Vegan Cakes

Prep time: 15 minutes | Cook time: 15minutes |
Serves 8

- 4 potatoes, diced and boiled
- 1 bunch green onions
- 1 lime, zest, and juice
- 1½ inch knob of fresh ginger
- 1 tablespoon tamari
- 4 tablespoons red curry paste
- 4 sheets nori
- 1 (398 grams) can heart of palm, drained
- ¾ cup canned artichoke hearts, drained
- Black pepper, to taste
- Salt, to taste

1. Add potatoes, green onions, lime zest, juice, and the rest of the ingredients to a food processor.
2. Press the pulse button and blend until smooth.
3. Make 8 small patties out of this mixture.
4. Place the patties in the air fryer basket.
5. Transfer the basket to the 3rd rack position of Ninja Foodi XL Pro Air Oven and close the door.
6. Select the "Air Fry" Mode using the Function Keys and select Rack Level 3.
7. Set its cooking time to 15 minutes and temperature to 400 degrees F, then press "START/STOP" to initiate cooking.
8. Serve warm.

Vegetable Casserole

Prep time: 15 minutes | Cook time: 42 minutes | Serves 6

- 2 cups peas
- 8 ounces mushrooms, sliced
- 4 tablespoons all-purpose flour
- 1 ½ cups celery, sliced
- 1 ½ cups carrots, sliced
- ½ teaspoon mustard powder
- 2 cups milk
- salt and black pepper, to taste
- 7 tablespoons butter
- 1 cup breadcrumbs
- ½ cup Parmesan cheese, grated

1. Grease and rub a casserole dish with butter and keep it aside.
2. Add carrots, onion, and celery to a saucepan, then fill it with water.
3. Cover this pot and cook for 10 minutes, then stir in peas.
4. Cook for 4 minutes, then strain the vegetables.
5. Now melt 1 tablespoon of butter in the same saucepan and toss in mushrooms to sauté.
6. Once the mushrooms are soft, transfer them to the vegetables.
7. Prepare the sauce by melting 4 tablespoons of butter in a suitable saucepan.
8. Stir in mustard and flour, then stir cook for 2 minutes
9. Gradually pour in the milk and stir cook until thickened, then add salt and black pepper.
10. Add vegetables and mushrooms to the flour milk mixture and mix well.
11. Spread this vegetable blend in the casserole dish evenly.
12. Toss the breadcrumbs with the remaining butter and spread it on top of vegetables.
13. Top this casserole dish with cheese.
14. Transfer the dish to the Ninja Foodi Digital Air Fry Oven and close the door.
15. Select "Air Fry" mode by rotating the dial.
16. Press the TIME/SLICE button and change the value to 25 minutes
17. Press the TEMP/DARKNESS button and change the value to 350 degrees F.
18. Press Start/Pause to begin cooking.
19. Serve warm.

Baked Vegetables

Prep time: 5 minutes | Cook time: 35 minutes |Serves 4

- 3 cups Brussels sprouts, cut in half
- 2 zucchini, cut into 1/2-inch slices
- 2 bell peppers, cut into 2-inch chunks
- 8 oz mushrooms, cut in half
- 1 onion, cut into wedges
- 2 tbsp vinegar
- 1/4 cup olive oil
- 1/2 tsp salt

1. Add vegetables into the zip-lock bag. Mix together vinegar, oil, and salt and pour over vegetables.
2. Seal zip-lock bag and shake well and place it in the refrigerator for 1 hour.
3. Spread vegetables on a sheet pan.
4. Select bake mode then set the temperature to 375 F and time for 35 minutes. Press start.
5. Once the oven is preheated then place the sheet pan into the oven.
6. Serve and enjoy.

Roast Cauliflower and Broccoli

Prep time: 15 minutes | Cook time: 10 minutes | Serves 4

- ½ pound broccoli, florets
- ½ pound cauliflower, florets
- 1 tablespoon olive oil
- Black pepper, to taste
- Salt, to taste
- ⅓ cup water

1. Toss all the veggies with seasoning in a large bowl.
2. Spread these vegetables in the air fryer basket.
3. Transfer the basket to the 3rd rack position of Ninja Foodi XL Pro Air Oven and close the door.
4. Select the "Air Fry" Mode using the Function Keys and select Rack Level 3.
5. Set its cooking time to 10 minutes and temperature to 400 degrees F, then press "START/STOP" to initiate cooking.
6. Serve warm.

Blue Cheese Soufflés

Prep time: 15 minutes | Cook time: 17minutes | Serves 4

- 2 ounces unsalted butter
- 1-ounce breadcrumbs
- 1-ounce plain flour
- Pinch English mustard powder
- Pinch cayenne pepper
- 10 ounces semi-skimmed milk
- 3 ounces blue murder cheese
- 1 fresh thyme sprig, chopped
- 4 medium eggs, separated

1. Grease four ramekins with butter and sprinkle with breadcrumbs.
2. Melt butter in a suitable saucepan, stir in flour, cayenne, and mustard powder.
3. Then mix well and cook for 1 minute, then slowly pour in the milk.
4. Mix well until smooth, then boil its sauce. Cook for 2 minutes.
5. Stir in cheese, and mix well until melted.
6. Add black pepper, salt, and egg yolks.
7. Beat egg whites in a bowl with a mixer until they make stiff peaks.
8. Add egg whites to the cheese sauce, then mix well.
9. Divide the mixture into the ramekins and transfer to the Ninja Foodi XL Pro Air Oven, then close its door.
10. Select the "Air Fry" Mode using the Function Keys and select Rack Level 2.
11. Set its cooking time to 14 minutes and temperature to 350 degrees F, then press "START/STOP" to initiate cooking.
12. Serve warm.

Cauliflower Tots

Prep time: 5 minutes | Cook time: 10 minutes |Serves 4

- Cooking spray
- 450g cauliflower tots

1. Using nonstick cooking spray, coat the air fry basket.
2. Place as many cauliflower tots as you can in the air fry basket, ensuring sure they do not touch, and air fry in batches if needed.
3. Turn on Ninja Foodi Dual Heat Air Fry Oven and rotate the knob to select "Air Fry".
4. Select the timer for 6 minutes and the temperature for 400 degrees F.
5. Pull the basket out, flip the tots, and cook for another 3 minutes, or until browned and cooked through.
6. Remove from Ninja Foodi Dual Heat Air Fry Oven to serve.

Soy Sauce Green Beans

Prep time: 10 minutes | Cook time: 10 minutes | Serves 2

- 8 ounces fresh green beans, trimmed and cut in half
- 1 tablespoon soy sauce
- 1 teaspoon sesame oil

1. In a bowl, mix together the green beans, soy sauce and sesame oil.
2. Press "Power" button of Ninja Foodi Digital Air Fry Oven and turn the dial to select "Air Fry" mode.
3. Press TIME/SLICE button and again turn the dial to set the cooking time to 10 minutes
4. Now push TEMP/DARKNESS button and rotate the dial to set the temperature at 390 degrees F.
5. Press "Start/Pause" button to start.
6. When the unit beeps to show that it is preheated, open the oven door.
7. Arrange the green beans in air fry basket and insert in the oven.
8. When cooking time is completed, open the oven door and serve hot.

Caramelized Baby Carrots

Prep time: 10 minutes | Cook time: 15 minutes | Serves 4

- ½ cup butter, melted
- ½ cup brown sugar
- 1 pound bag baby carrots

1. In a bowl, mix the butter, brown sugar and carrots together.
2. Press "Power Button" of Ninja Foodi XL Pro Air Oven and select "Air Fry" function.
3. Press "Temp Button" to set the temperature at 400 degrees F.

4. Now press "Time Button" to set the cooking time to 15 minutes.
5. Press "START/STOP" button to start.
6. When the unit beeps to show that it is preheated, open the lid.
7. Arrange the carrots in a greased air fry basket and insert in the oven.
8. When cooking time is completed, open the lid and serve warm.

Sweet Potato Casserole

Prep time: 15 minutes | Cook time: 35 minutes | Serves 6

- 3 cups sweet potatoes, mashed and cooled
- 1 ½ cups brown sugar, packed
- 2 large eggs, beaten
- 1 teaspoon vanilla extract
- ½ cup milk
- ¾ cup butter, melted
- ⅓ cup flour
- 4 ounces pecans, chopped

1. Mix the sweet potato mash with vanilla extract, milk, eggs, 1 cup of brown sugar, and ½ cup of melted butter in a large bowl.
2. Spread this sweet potato mixture in a casserole dish.
3. Now whisk remaining sugar and butter with flour in a separate bowl.
4. Fold in pecan, then top the sweet potatoes mixed with this pecan mixture.
5. Transfer the dish to the Ninja Foodi Digital Air Fry Oven and close the door.
6. Select "Bake" mode by rotating the dial.
7. Press the TIME/SLICE button and change the value to 35 minutes
8. Press the TEMP/DARKNESS button and change the value to 350 degrees F.
9. Press Start/Pause to begin cooking.
10. Slice and serve!

Brussels Sprouts Gratin

Prep time: 15 minutes | Cook time: 35 minutes | Serves 6

- 1 pound Brussels sprouts
- 1 garlic clove, cut in half
- 3 tablespoons butter, divided
- 2 tablespoons shallots, minced
- 2 tablespoons all-purpose flour
- Kosher salt, to taste
- freshly ground black pepper
- 1 cup milk
- ½ cup fontina cheese, shredded
- 1 strip of bacon, cooked and crumbled
- ½ cup fine bread crumbs

1. Trim the Brussels sprouts and remove their outer leaves.
2. Slice the sprouts into quarters, then rinse them under cold water.
3. Grease a gratin dish with cooking spray and rub it with garlic halves.
4. Boil salted water in a suitable pan, then add Brussels sprouts.
5. Cook the sprouts for 3 minutes, then immediately drain.
6. Place a suitable saucepan over medium-low heat and melt 2 tablespoons of butter in it.
7. Toss in shallots and sauté until soft, then stir in flour, nutmeg, ½ teaspoons of salt, and black pepper.
8. Stir cook for 2 minutes, then gradually add milk and a half and half cream.
9. Mix well and add bacon along with shredded cheese.
10. Fold in Brussels sprouts and transfer this mixture to the casserole dish.
11. Toss breadcrumbs with 1 tablespoon butter and spread over the casserole.
12. Transfer the gratin to the Ninja Foodi Digital Air Fry Oven and close the door.
13. Select "Bake" mode by rotating the dial.
14. Press the TIME/SLICE button and change the value to 25 minutes
15. Press the TEMP/DARKNESS button and change the value to 350 degrees F.
16. Press Start/Pause to begin cooking.
17. Enjoy!

Spicy Brussels Sprouts

Prep time: 5 minutes | Cook time: 30 minutes |Serves 6

- 2 cups Brussels sprouts, halved
- 1/4 tsp garlic powder
- 1/4 cup olive oil
- 1/4 tsp cayenne
- 1/4 tsp chili powder
- 1/4 tsp salt

1. Add all ingredients into the large bowl and toss well.
2. Transfer Brussels sprouts on a sheet pan.
3. Select bake mode then set the temperature to 400 F and time for 30 minutes. Press start.
4. Once the oven is preheated then place the baking dish into the oven.
5. Stir Brussels sprouts halfway through.
6. Serve and enjoy.

Fried Tortellini

Prep time: 15 minutes | Cook time: 10 minutes | Serves 8

- 1 (9-ounces) package cheese tortellini
- 1 cup Panko breadcrumbs
- ⅓ cup Parmesan, grated
- 1 teaspoon dried oregano
- ½ teaspoon garlic powder
- ½ teaspoon crushed red pepper flakes
- Kosher salt, to taste
- Freshly ground black pepper, to taste
- 1 cup all-purpose flour
- 2 large eggs

1. Boil tortellini according to salted boiling water according to package's instructions, then drain.
2. Mix panko with garlic powder, black pepper, salt, red pepper flakes, oregano, Parmesan in a small bowl.
3. Beat eggs in one bowl and spread flour on a plate.
4. Coat the tortellini with the flour, dip into the eggs and then coat with the panko mixture.
5. Spread the tortellini in the air fryer basket and spray them with cooking oil.
6. Transfer the basket to the 3rd rack position of Ninja Foodi XL Pro Air Oven and close the door.
7. Select the "Air Fry" Mode using the Function Keys and select Rack Level 3.
8. Set its cooking time to 10 minutes and temperature to 400 degrees F, then press "START/STOP" to initiate cooking.
9. Serve warm.

Wine Braised Mushrooms

Prep time: 10 minutes | Cook time: 32 minutes | Serves 6

- 1 tablespoon butter
- 2 teaspoons Herbs de Provence
- ½ teaspoon garlic powder
- 2 pounds fresh mushrooms, quartered
- 2 tablespoons white wine

1. In a frying pan, mix together the butter, Herbs de Provence, and garlic powder over medium-low heat and stir fry for about 2 minutes
2. Stir in the mushrooms and remove from the heat.
3. Transfer the mushroom mixture into a sheet pan.
4. Press "Power" button of Ninja Foodi Digital Air Fry Oven and turn the dial to select "Air Fry" mode.
5. Press TIME/SLICE button and again turn the dial to set the cooking time to 30 minutes
6. Now push TEMP/DARKNESS button and rotate the dial to set the temperature at 320 degrees F.
7. Press "Start/Pause" button to start.
8. When the unit beeps to show that it is preheated, open the oven door.
9. Arrange the pan over the wire rack and insert in the oven.
10. After 25 minutes of cooking, stir the wine into mushroom mixture.
11. When cooking time is completed, open the oven door and serve hot.

Asparagus With Garlic And Parmesan

Prep time: 5 minutes | Cook time: 10 minutes |Serves 4

- 1 bundle asparagus
- 1 teaspoon olive oil
- 1/8 teaspoon garlic salt
- 1 tablespoon parmesan cheese
- Pepper to taste

1. Clean the asparagus and dry it. To remove the woody stalks, cut 1 inch off the bottom.
2. In a SearPlate, arrange asparagus in a single layer and spray with oil.
3. Turn on Ninja Foodi Dual Heat Air Fry Oven and rotate the knob to select "Air Fry".
4. Select the timer for 10 minutes and the temperature for 350 degrees F.
5. Enjoy right away.

Creamy Cauliflower Hummus

Prep time: 5 minutes | Cook time: 35 minutes |Serves 8

- 1 cauliflower head, cut into florets
- 2 tbsp fresh lime juice
- 1 tsp garlic, chopped
- 1/3 cup tahini
- 3 tbsp olive oil
- Pepper
- Salt

1. Spread cauliflower onto the sheet pan.
2. Select bake mode then set the temperature to 400 F and time for 35 minutes. Press start.
3. Once the oven is preheated then place the sheet pan into the oven.
4. Transfer cauliflower into the food processor. Add remaining ingredients and process until smooth.
5. Serve and enjoy.

Cheesy Green Bean Casserole

Prep time: 5 minutes | Cook time: 35 minutes |Serves 6

- 4 cups green beans, cooked and chopped
- 3 tablespoons butter
- 8 ounces mushrooms, sliced
- ¼ cup onion, chopped
- 2 tablespoons flour
- 1 teaspoon salt
- ¼ teaspoon ground black pepper
- 1 ½ cups milk
- 2 cups cheddar cheese, shredded
- 2 tablespoons sour cream
- 1 cup soft breadcrumbs
- 2 tablespoons butter, melted
- ¼ cup Parmesan cheese, grated
- 1 cup French fried onions

1. Add butter to a suitable saucepan and melt it over medium-low heat.
2. Toss in onion and mushrooms, then sauté until soft.
3. Stir in flour, salt, and black pepper. Mix well, then slowly pour in the milk.
4. Stir in sour cream, green beans, and cheddar cheese, then cook until it thickens.
5. Transfer this green bean mixture to a SearPlate and spread it evenly.
6. Toss breadcrumbs with fried onion and butter.
7. Top the mixture with this bread crumbs mixture.
8. Transfer the dish to Ninja Foodi Dual Heat Air Fry Oven and close the door.
9. Select "Bake" mode by rotating the dial.
10. Press the TIME/SLICES button and change the value to 25 minutes.
11. Press the TEMP/SHADE button and change the value to 350 degrees F.
12. Press Start/Stop to begin cooking.
13. Serve and enjoy!

Chapter 8

Dessert Recipes

Air Fried Churros

Prep time: 5 minutes | Cook time: 12 minutes |Serves 8

- 1 cup water
- ⅓ cup butter, cut into cubes
- 2 tablespoons granulated sugar
- ¼ teaspoon salt
- 1 cup all-purpose flour
- 2 large eggs
- 1 teaspoon vanilla extract
- oil spray
- Cinnamon Coating:
- ½ cup granulated sugar
- ¾ teaspoons ground cinnamon

1. Grease the SearPlate with cooking spray.
2. Warm water with butter, salt, and sugar in a suitable saucepan until it boils.
3. Now reduce its heat, then slowly stir in flour and mix well until smooth.
4. Remove the mixture from the heat and leave it for 4 minutes to cool.
5. Add vanilla extract and eggs, then beat the mixture until it comes together as a batter.
6. Transfer this churro mixture to a piping bag with star-shaped tips and pipe the batter on the prepared SearPlate to get 4-inch churros using this batter.
7. Refrigerate these churros for 1 hour, then transfer them to the Air fry sheet.
8. Transfer the SearPlate into Ninja Foodi Dual Heat Air Fry Oven and close the door.
9. Select "Air Fry" mode by rotating the dial.
10. Press the TEMP/SHADE button and change the value to 375 degrees F.
11. Press the TIME/SLICES button and change the value to 12 minutes, then press Start/Stop to begin cooking.
12. Meanwhile, mix granulated sugar with cinnamon in a bowl.
13. Drizzle this mixture over the air fried churros.
14. Serve.

Dehydrated Pineapple

Prep time: 5 minutes | Cook time: 12 hours |Serves 2

- 1 cup pineapple chunks

1. Select dehydrate mode, set temperature to 135 F, and set timer to 12 hours.
2. Place pineapple chunks in the air fryer basket and place basket into top rails of the oven. Close door.

Zucchini Chips

Prep time: 5 minutes | Cook time: 10 hours |Serves 4

- 4 cups zucchini slices
- 3 tbsp BBQ sauce

1. Add zucchini slices into the bowl. Pour BBQ sauce over zucchini slices and mix well.
2. Arrange zucchini slices in an air fryer basket and place the basket in the oven.
3. Select dehydrate then set the temperature to 135 F and time to 10 hours. Press start.
4. Store in a container.

Cherry Jam Tarts

Prep time: 5 minutes | Cook time: 40 minutes |Serves 6

- 2 sheets shortcrust pastry
- For the frangipane
- 4 ounces butter softened
- 4 ounces golden caster sugar
- 1 egg
- 1 tablespoon plain flour
- 4 ounces ground almonds
- 3 ounces cherry jam
- For the icing
- 1 cup icing sugar
- 12 glacé cherries

1. Grease the 12 cups of the muffin tray with butter.
2. Roll the puff pastry into a 10 cm sheet, then cut 12 rounds out of it.
3. Place these rounds into each muffin cup and press them into these cups.
4. Transfer the muffin tray to the refrigerator and leave it for 20 minutes.
5. Add dried beans or pulses into each tart crust to add weight.
6. Transfer the muffin tray on wire rack in Ninja Foodi Dual Heat Air Fry Oven and close the door.
7. Select "Bake" mode by rotating the dial.
8. Press the TIME/SLICES button and change the value to 10 minutes.
9. Press the TEMP/SHADE button and change the value to 350 degrees F.
10. Press Start/Stop to begin cooking.
11. Now remove the dried beans from the crust and bake again for 10 minutes in Ninja Foodi Dual Heat Air Fry Oven.
12. Meanwhile, prepare the filling beat, beat butter with sugar and egg until fluffy.
13. Stir in flour and almonds ground, then mix well.
14. Divide this filling in the baked crusts and top them with a tablespoon of cherry jam.
15. Now again, place the muffin tray in Ninja Foodi Dual Heat Air Fry Oven.
16. Continue cooking on the "Bake" mode for 20 minutes at 350 degrees F.
17. Whisk the icing sugar with 2 tablespoons water and top the baked tarts with sugar mixture.
18. Serve.

Broiled Bananas With Cream

Prep time: 5 minutes | Cook time: 10 minutes |Serves 3

- 3 large bananas, ripe
- 2 tablespoons dark brown sugar
- ⅔ cup heavy cream
- 1 pinch flaky salt

1. Slice the bananas thickly.
2. Arrange in the SearPlate, gently overlapping.
3. Sprinkle the brown sugar evenly on top, followed by the cream and then the salt.
4. Turn on Ninja Foodi Dual Heat Air Fry Oven and rotate the knob to select "Broil".
5. Select the unit for 7 minutes at HI.
6. When the unit beeps to signify it has preheated, open the oven door and insert the SearPlate.
7. Close the oven and cook until the cream has thickened, browned, and become spotty.
8. Allow cooling for two minutes before serving.

Scalloped Pineapple

Prep time: 5 minutes | Cook time: 30 minutes |Serves 6

- 3 eggs, lightly beaten
- 1/2 cup butter, melted
- 8 oz can pineapple, crushed
- 1 1/2 cups sugar
- 1/2 cup brown sugar
- 4 cups of bread cubes
- 1/4 cup milk

1. In a large bowl, combine together eggs, milk, butter, brown sugar, pineapple, and sugar.
2. Add bread cubes and stir until well coated.
3. Pour mixture into the greased baking dish.
4. Select bake mode then set the temperature to 350 F and time for 30 minutes. Press start.
5. Once the oven is preheated then place the baking dish into the oven.
6. Serve and enjoy.

Chocolate Oatmeal Cookies

Prep time: 5 minutes | Cook time: 10 minutes |Serves 36

- 3 cups quick-cooking oatmeal
- 1½ cups all-purpose flour
- ½ cup cream
- ¼ cup cocoa powder
- ¾ cup white sugar
- 1 package instant chocolate pudding mix
- 1 teaspoon baking soda
- 1 teaspoon salt
- 1 cup butter, softened
- ¾ cup brown sugar
- 2 eggs
- 1 teaspoon vanilla extract
- 2 cups chocolate chips
- Cooking spray

1. Using parchment paper, line the air fry basket.
2. Using nonstick cooking spray, coat the air fry basket.
3. Combine the oats, flour, cocoa powder, pudding mix, baking soda, and salt in a mixing dish. Set aside.
4. Mix cream, butter, brown sugar, and white sugar in a separate bowl using an electric mixer.
5. Combine the eggs and vanilla essence in a mixing bowl. Mix in the oatmeal mixture thoroughly. Mix the chocolate chips and walnuts in a bowl.
6. Using a large cookie scoop, drop dough into the air fry basket; level out and leave about 1 inch between each cookie.
7. Turn on Ninja Foodi Dual Heat Air Fry Oven and rotate the knob to select "Air Fry".
8. Select the timer for 10 minutes and the temperature for 350 degrees F.
9. Before serving, cool on a wire rack.

Nutritious Almonds

Prep time: 5 minutes | Cook time: 12 hours |Serves 4

- 1 cup almonds, soaked in water for overnight
- 1/4 tsp cayenne
- 1/2 tbsp olive oil

1. Toss almonds with oil and cayenne.
2. Spread almonds in an air fryer basket and place the basket in the oven.
3. Select dehydrate then set the temperature to 125 F and time to 12 hours. Press start.
4. Store in a container.

Delicious Cashew Blondies

Prep time: 5 minutes | Cook time: 40 minutes |Serves 16

- 2 eggs
- 1 1/2 cups all-purpose flour
- 1 cup cashews, roasted & chopped
- 1 tbsp vanilla
- 2 cups brown sugar
- 1 cup butter, softened
- 1 tsp baking powder
- 1 tsp salt

1. In a bowl, mix together flour, baking powder, and salt and set aside.
2. In a separate bowl, beat butter and sugar until light. Add eggs and vanilla and beat until well combined.
3. Add flour mixture and mix well.
4. Add cashews and stir well.
5. Pour mixture into the greased baking pan.
6. Select bake mode then set the temperature to 350 F and time for 40 minutes. Press start.
7. Once the oven is preheated then place the baking dish into the oven.
8. Slice and serve.

Sweet Mango Slices

Prep time: 5 minutes | Cook time: 12 hours |Serves 2

- 2 mangoes, peel and cut into 1/4-inch thick slices
- 1/2 tbsp honey
- 2 tbsp lime juice

1. In a bowl, mix together lime juice and honey.
2. Add mango slices and coat well.
3. Arrange mango slices in an air fryer basket and place the basket in the oven.
4. Select dehydrate then set the temperature to 135 F and time to 12 hours. Press start.
5. Store in a container.

Ricotta Cake

Prep time: 5 minutes | Cook time: 55 minutes |Serves 8

- 4 eggs
- 18 oz ricotta cheese
- 1 fresh lemon zest
- 2 tablespoon stevia
- 1 fresh lemon juice

1. In a large bowl, whisk the ricotta with an electric mixer until smooth.
2. Add egg one by one and whisk well. Add lemon juice, lemon zest, and stevia and mix well. Transfer mixture into the prepared cake pan.
3. Place the wire rack inside.
4. Select "BAKE" mode, set the temperature to 350 degrees F, and set time to 55 minutes.
5. Press "START/PAUSE" to begin preheating. Once the oven is preheated, place the cake pan on a wire rack and close the oven door to start cooking. Cook for 55 minutes.
6. Place cake in the refrigerator for 1-2 hours.
7. Cut into the slices and serve.

Pear Slices

Prep time: 5 minutes | Cook time: 5 hours |Serves 4

- 2 pears, cut into 1/4-inch thick slices

1. Select dehydrate mode, set temperature to 160 F, and set timer to 5 hours.
2. Place pear slices in the air fryer basket and place basket into top rails of the oven. Close door.

Dehydrated Raspberries

Prep time: 5 minutes | Cook time: 12 hours |Serves 4

- 2 cups fresh raspberries, wash and pat dry with a paper towel

1. Select dehydrate mode, set temperature to 135 F, and set timer to 12 hours.
2. Place raspberries in the air fryer basket and place basket into top rails of the oven. Close door.

Beef Jerky

Prep time: 5 minutes | Cook time: 8 hours |Serves 4

- 1 lb flank steak, cut into thin slices
- 1 1/2 tbsp ranch seasoning
- 1/2 cup Worcestershire sauce
- 1/4 tsp cayenne
- 1 tsp liquid smoke
- 1 tbsp chili flakes
- 1/2 cup soy sauce

1. Add all ingredients into the large bowl and mix well.
2. Cover and place in the refrigerator overnight.
3. Arrange meat slices in an air fryer basket and place the basket in the oven.
4. Select dehydrate then set the temperature to 145 F and time to 8 hours. Press start.
5. Store in a container.

Strawberry Slices

Prep time: 5 minutes | Cook time: 12 hours |Serves 3

- 1 cup strawberries, cut into 1/8-inch thick slices

1. Arrange strawberry slices in an air fryer basket and place the basket in the oven.
2. Select dehydrate then set the temperature to 130 F and time to 12 hours. Press start.
3. Store in a container.

Dehydrated Chickpeas

Prep time: 5 minutes | Cook time: 10 hours |Serves 4

- 14 oz can chickpeas, drained and rinsed
- Salt

1. Select dehydrate mode, set temperature to 135 F, and set timer to 10 hours.
2. Place chickpeas in the air fryer basket and season with salt.
3. Place basket into top rails of the oven. Close door.

Appendix 1 Measurement Conversion Chart

Volume Equivalents (Dry)	
US STANDARD	**METRIC (APPROXIMATE)**
1/8 teaspoon	0.5 mL
1/4 teaspoon	1 mL
1/2 teaspoon	2 mL
3/4 teaspoon	4 mL
1 teaspoon	5 mL
1 tablespoon	15 mL
1/4 cup	59 mL
1/2 cup	118 mL
3/4 cup	177 mL
1 cup	235 mL
2 cups	475 mL
3 cups	700 mL
4 cups	1 L

Volume Equivalents (Liquid)		
US STANDARD	**US STANDARD (OUNCES)**	**METRIC (AP-PROXIMATE)**
2 tablespoons	1 fl.oz.	30 mL
1/4 cup	2 fl.oz.	60 mL
1/2 cup	4 fl.oz.	120 mL
1 cup	8 fl.oz.	240 mL
1 1/2 cup	12 fl.oz.	355 mL
2 cups or 1 pint	16 fl.oz.	475 mL
4 cups or 1 quart	32 fl.oz.	1 L
1 gallon	128 fl.oz.	4 L

Temperatures Equivalents	
FAHRENHEIT(F)	**CELSIUS(C) APPROXIMATE**
225 °F	107 °C
250 °F	120 ° °C
275 °F	135 °C
300 °F	150 °C
325 °F	160 °C
350 °F	180 °C
375 °F	190 °C
400 °F	205 °C
425 °F	220 °C
450 °F	235 °C
475 °F	245 °C
500 °F	260 °C

Weight Equivalents	
US STANDARD	**METRIC (APPROXIMATE)**
1 ounce	28 g
2 ounces	57 g
5 ounces	142 g
10 ounces	284 g
15 ounces	425 g
16 ounces (1 pound)	455 g
1.5 pounds	680 g
2 pounds	907 g

Appendix 2 The Dirty Dozen and Clean Fifteen

The Environmental Working Group (EWG) is a nonprofit, nonpartisan organization dedicated to protecting human health and the environment Its mission is to empower people to live healthier lives in a healthier environment. This organization publishes an annual list of the twelve kinds of produce, in sequence, that have the highest amount of pesticide residue-the Dirty Dozen-as well as a list of the fifteen kinds ofproduce that have the least amount of pesticide residue-the Clean Fifteen.

THE DIRTY DOZEN

The 2016 Dirty Dozen includes the following produce. These are considered among the year's most important produce to buy organic:

Strawberries	Spinach
Apples	Tomatoes
Nectarines	Bell peppers
Peaches	Cherry tomatoes
Celery	Cucumbers
Grapes	Kale/collard greens
Cherries	Hot peppers

The Dirty Dozen list contains two additional itemskale/collard greens and hot peppers-because they tend to contain trace levels of highly hazardous pesticides.

THE CLEAN FIFTEEN

The least critical to buy organically are the Clean Fifteen list. The following are on the 2016 list:

Avocados	Papayas
Corn	Kiw
Pineapples	Eggplant
Cabbage	Honeydew
Sweet peas	Grapefruit
Onions	Cantaloupe
Asparagus	Cauliflower
Mangos	

Some of the sweet corn sold in the United States are made from genetically engineered (GE) seedstock. Buy organic varieties of these crops to avoid GE produce.

Appendix 3 Index

Cassandra A. Hoffman

Printed in Great Britain
by Amazon

31048588R00044